For my best friend Kathy and my two inspirational
kids, Sierra and Luke.

WWW.HELPCOACHKIDS.COM

ISBN-13: 978-1478184270
ISBN-10: 1478184272

CONTENTS

1. INTRODUCTION

CONGRATULATIONS!

You have volunteered to be a youth coach. You have made a significant commitment to help shape the characters of kids and to enrich their lives. This should be considered a great honor as well as a great responsibility. For many kids you will be the first person to introduce them to organized sports. Therefore, it is critical that you lay the proper foundation for learning and enjoyment.

Let the kids provide the expectations and leave your win-at-all-cost attitude outside the gym. You are there to provide the knowledge of the game and the necessary environment, structure and activities to help develop the kids into better people and players. You will use the simple teaching tools and practice plans in this guidebook to take the kids through structured drills and exercises to help improve their health and skill level and develop their competitive drive. Along the way, you will teach them the fundamentals of basketball with sportsmanship and effort as the foundation. By following the basic principles in this guidebook you will ensure a healthy and fulfilling experience for the kids, the parents and yourself.

IT'S ALL ABOUT THE KIDS

Approximately 40 million kids participate in youth sports each year under the supervision of about 4 million youth coaches. Numerous surveys have been conducted on the reasons why kids participate in sports and the conclusions are quite revealing: having fun is consistently at or near the top of the list of reasons, while winning is consistently at or near the bottom of the list. The game belongs to the kids....let them play.

While initial participation by kids is robust and their motives are pure, there is a growing crisis in youth sports. An estimated 30% of kids quit playing organized sports each year and 70% of all kids stop playing by the age of 13. Not surprisingly, the main reason given by kids for dropping out of sports is the lack of fun or the lack of interest, followed closely by poor coaching. The worst thing you can do as a youth coach is take away a child's desire to play sports. But, that is exactly what has been occurring at an increasing rate year after year.

1

> *"Kind words can be short and easy to speak, but their echoes are endless." -- Mother Teresa*

The solution is clear and is well supported by research – 96% of kids playing sports return to play the following year when they are coached using an overwhelmingly positive and knowledgeable approach. It is up to today's youth coaches to learn from the mistakes made by their predecessors and infuse as much fun and positivity as possible into each practice and game. You can either contribute to the problem or help solve the problem. Following the basic principles of this guidebook will help fulfill your obligation to ensure the happiness and well being of your players.

This positive concept is not new. Legendary coach, John Wooden, was a major proponent and practitioner of positive coaching. He was a mild mannered leader who believed strongly in the power of praise and encouragement. He used criticism sparingly and rarely raised his voice. If his positive approach was able to motivate college players to win 10 NCAA Championships, it should be the only approach considered for coaching kids in elementary school. Coach Wooden would be the first one to tell you that the wins were not nearly as important as the growth and development of his player's characters, and that the effort to win was much more important than the outcome. His record is a testament to the fact that positive energy leads to better performance on and off the court – winning is merely a byproduct.

Following this guidebook is a good start to becoming a better youth coach. However, every youth coach should seek training and education from a certified coaching organization such as the National Youth Sports Coaches Association, the National Alliance for Youth Sports, or the Positive Coaching Alliance. They should also take advantage of any training their league may provide.

2. THE PRE-SEASON CHECKLIST

You're the new coach...now what?

1. Thoroughly review your league rules and regulations.
2. Call the parents of the kids on your roster to simply introduce yourself and to answer any questions they may have.
3. Once the final roster has been set, email the parents to provide some basic information. The email should include:
   - Your name, contact information and a brief bio.
   - The names of the kids on your roster.
   - The initial practice date/time and location (if known).
   - The game schedule (if known).
   - Basic equipment and clothing requirements for the kids (ball size, non-marking athletic shoes, etc.).
   - Information about uniforms.
   - You can request 1 or 2 volunteers to act as assistant coaches.
   - Ask parents to send you any relevant medical conditions or special requirements for their child (diabetes, asthma, etc.).
   - Request that at least one parent stay for the first 15-20 minutes of the first practice for a brief meeting. The meeting is outlined in the "Working With Parents" section (pg. 17).
4. Send subsequent emails with any new or updated information.
5. Prior to the first practice put together the following coaches "kit":
   - A basic first aid kit: band aids, instant cold compress, antiseptic/pain relieving spray (works wonders on floor burns).
   - A blank incident report (see "Safety" pg. 4).
   - A list of the kids on your team along with their parent's names and contact information.
   - The practice and game schedule (as soon as they are available).
   - Your league's contact information, including the weather hotline.
   - The wristbands explained in the "Wristband Method" (pg. 62).
   - 6-10 cones for drills.
   - A small pump and needle to inflate balls.
   - A clipboard with a court diagram and marker.
   - Mints/mint gum (kids listen better when your breath is fresh).

PART 1: COACHING KIDS

Coaching is teaching through sports. Good youth coaches teach kids how to better play, compete, and behave. Good youth coaches lead by example through their words and actions. Good youth coaches are knowledgeable and passionate about their sport. Good youth coaches care about their players and treat them fairly. Good youth coaches are good communicators. Good youth coaches care more about developing winning kids than kids that win.

Coaching kids involves 9 basic elements within the following three categories: 1) The Three Mandatory Requirements of Coaching Kids, 2) The Three Principles for Improvement, 3) The Three Unavoidable Difficulties.

3. THE THREE MANDATORY REQUIREMENTS

1. SAFETY

Youth coaches must ensure the physical and emotional safety of the kids while they are in their care. Some of the things to remember that can help ensure a safe and healthy environment are:

- Don't allow the kids to push, trip, tackle, grab, or hit one another;
- Don't allow the kids to tease, criticize, or bully one another;
- Don't allow the kids to use bad language or yell in anger;
- Don't allow the kids to climb on or misuse fixtures and equipment;
- Don't allow the kids to throw balls at one another;
- Quickly remove any water or debris from the floor.

Other things you should and should not do:

- ➤ NEVER verbally or physically abuse kids while they are in your care. NEVER curse at them, yell in anger at them, embarrass or humiliate them, threaten them; and NEVER touch them unless you are giving a high five or patting their head. NEVER allow others to do any of these things to the kids while they are in your care.
- ➤ Don't drink alcohol are take illegal drugs prior to or while working with kids.
- ➤ Don't smoke while working with kids.

➢ Bring a basic first aid kit to every practice and game.

➢ In the unlikely event of a serious injury, call 911 (especially for head and neck injuries) and then call the parents. You should also have a blank incident report to document the accident. Your league should be able to provide this document.

➢ You should familiarize yourself with the closest emergency care facilities, and keep a list of the kids on your team along with the names and contact information of their parents.

➢ Consider getting CPR certification. It's a skill worth knowing even when not coaching.

➢ Ask parents if their kids have any special medical or emotional conditions (diabetes, asthma, etc.) that you need to be aware of, and get some basic instructions on how to deal with them.

➢ Keep in mind that kids get hot faster than adults and stay hot longer than adults. Make sure you are giving them an adequate number of water breaks during practice and games.

➢ You must ensure that each child is picked up by a parent or guardian after each practice and game. Don't leave any child unattended.

2. FUN & POSITIVE

Youth coaches must ensure a fun and positive experience for the kids. It cannot be overstated: participating in youth sports should be all about having fun -- for everyone. Kids simply want unconditional support and encouragement from their youth coaches. Expressing these positive attitudes only when kids win or perform perfectly sends the wrong message and sets up a conditional relationship that is unhealthy and unsustainable. Show them you care at all times. Kids only care about what their coach says when they know their coach cares about them.

The good news is that kids bring a playful attitude to the team from the beginning. It's up to youth coaches to help them maintain this positive attitude by creating a positive environment. Since the playing environment is a direct result of the youth coach's attitude, they should strive to feel, act and speak in a positive manner at all times. This can be difficult to do especially in the face of disappointment and adversity, but coaches need to constantly remind themselves that they are there for the kids and the kids just want to play sports and have fun. They have to trust that the learning, effort and improvements will follow as long as they maintain a fun and positive attitude.

Great youth coaches utilize a high praise to criticism ratio. The praise is always specific and sincere, and the criticism is never overly negative. Kids hear everything you say, but they hear negative criticism the loudest, and remember it the longest. Whenever possible, praise kids in front of the entire team as this will increase the player's self-esteem and it will teach the rest of the team what is worthy of praise. Abundant praise should not lead to coddling kids. Coddling can often do more harm than negative criticism by shielding kids from the lessons learned from experiencing adversity. Kids must endure struggles to learn and grow stronger.

3. <u>GOOD SPORTSMANSHIP</u>

Youth coaches must ensure that good sportsmanship is practiced at all times. Good character is the true measure of success in life and sportsmanship is the true measure of character in sports. Teaching kids good sportsmanship will provide life lessons that will prepare them for the more challenging aspects of life beyond sports. Good sportsmanship is all about acting and reacting in a positive and respectful manner. It's about maintaining composure and controlling negative emotions. It's about hard work and team work. It's about not being able to tell who won or lost after a game.

Sports don't build character, people build character. The quality of a child's adult leadership will determine the quality of the child. Great youth coaches do not sacrifice character development for athletic development. The first step in teaching kids good sportsmanship is to model such behavior yourself. Don't gloat or brag after wins, and don't sulk or get angry after losses. Teach your players to respect the sport, their opponents, their coaches, the officials, and the fans. Always remain positive and emphasize the enjoyment of playing the game and the development of the players and team.

Poor sportsmanship is never positive and has no place in youth sports. Unfortunately, kids by nature are immature and displays of poor sportsmanship are common. Kids will tease, brag, trash talk, ridicule, bully, lash out, and throw outrageous tantrums. These actions stem from their inability to control their emotions during moments of stress and excitement. As a youth coach you must immediately address displays of poor sportsmanship. Stop practice or call a timeout right away in order to explain what was done wrong and make it clear that such behavior will not be tolerated. Try not to embarrass individual players, but you will need to make it clear to the entire team what is and what is not acceptable.

4. THE THREE PRINCIPLES FOR IMPROVEMENT

1. PASSION & EXCITEMENT

Establishing a positive environment will allow passion and excitement to flow freely to and from kids. Passion is the internal spark that is necessary to ignite the motivation for kids to do something well. Effort, energy, and enthusiasm are the external expressions of passion that fuel kid's desire to compete. While enthusiasm cannot be taught, it can be encouraged and cultivated with the proper environment. Most kids walk into the gym already excited and enthusiastic about playing. Youth coaches need to harness that positive energy and get the kids to focus it on the skills and drills taught during practice and games. They will play hard without it feeling like work.

Good youth coaches bolster the kids natural level of excitement by being passionate and enthusiastic themselves – they fake it if necessary. Kids need large doses of positive feedback and reassurance to keep them excited. Youth coaches need to get out there on the court and really interact with the kids. They need to constantly encourage them to play hard and praise them when they give their best effort. Communicate loudly and with enthusiasm so the entire team can hear and join in the excitement. Use liberal doses of humor as well to keep the mood light and don't be stingy with the high fives and fist bumps. Your enthusiasm is essential to your success as a coach.

2. GOALS & EXPECTATIONS

Once kids show passion and excitement for sports, the youth coach must focus that energy on specific goals for improvements. Success is defined as setting a goal and reaching that goal. The goal of the youth coach should be to develop stronger and healthier kids in mind, body and spirit. Achieving this goal is the measure of success for the coach. The only expectations that should be imposed on the kids are to listen, have fun, play hard, and display good sportsmanship. Meeting these expectations is the measure of success for the kids – not winning.

The "Star Chart" system that is explained in detail later in this guidebook (pg. 71), gives kids concrete goals to strive for in a simple and fun tool. It is amazingly effective. The system involves coaches simply measuring the progress of each player within some basic basketball categories that every kid is familiar with. When kids show appropriate effort or improvement in one of the categories they are awarded a star. Their goal during the season is to earn stars for each of the categories identified by the coach. The measurement of progress is specific to each player, so the kids are competing against themselves to make improvements – not against each other. This reward system also takes the focus off of winning and places it on the kid's efforts to improve.

3. <u>EFFORT</u>

Effort is the work required to achieve goals. If you fuel kid's passion and excitement for a sport and give them obtainable goals to focus on, they will play hard and willingly give a vigorous effort. This is the ultimate measure of success for players and youth coaches. The score is absolutely meaningless when significant effort is put forth. Effort does not guarantee a win, but the lack of effort will almost always guarantee failure. Effort does not guarantee a flawless performance, but the lack of effort will guarantee mistakes. Be sure to enthusiastically praise the kids and the team when they make good efforts. You will reinforce and motivate the expected behavior.

For young kids, effort is a talent that is more important than athletic ability. Effort can be taught by expecting, encouraging and often insisting on hustle from your players. Don't allow kids to walk slowly on and off the court – have them run. Don't allow players to lazily go after loose balls and rebounds – teach them to go after the ball aggressively. Don't allow players to loaf on defense – constantly push them to get back on defense and guard their men. Don't even allow players to walk to team huddles. Push your kids to hustle at all times and praise them when they respond appropriately. If they don't hustle, have them run laps or do push-ups so they will learn what is expected. If the team does not hustle it is the fault of the youth coach, not the kids.

Competing is a willingness to put forth your best effort while going up against an opponent. It's a willingness to face a challenge head on. It's a willingness to fight through adversity and continue to play hard. Competing well is an acquired skill that consists of equal amounts of good sportsmanship and genuine effort. Like most things, kids do not treat competition as seriously as adults – nor should they. Placing kids in intensely competitive situations too early and too often can have a negative impact on their development as athletes and people. Give kids the freedom to compete on their own terms without the expectation of winning and the undue fear of losing constantly hovering over them. Emphasize the effort while competing, not the results of the competition.

THE FORMULA FOR SUCCESS

The common goal among players and coaches is that they both want visible improvements to be made in the quality of play. Therefore, success is measured on how well this goal is met. While an increase in effort is an achievement of success on its own, noticeable improvements almost always follow genuine effort. Effort is motivated by passion, which for kids is better described as excitement – and nothing excites kids more than positive feedback from someone with a positive attitude.

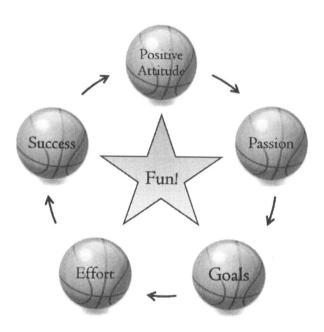

Therefore, success begins and ends with having a positive attitude -- and this positive attitude begins with the youth coach. When all of these elements are present, fun magically appears and success becomes inevitable. This is the case at every level of sports. Professional athletes unanimously agree that their best performances occur when they are having the most fun. This certainly holds true for kids.

5. THE THREE UNAVOIDABLE DIFFICULTIES

1. <u>DISCIPLINE</u>

The overwhelming theme of this guidebook is having fun and remaining positive. This does not suggest that there is no place for discipline when it comes to coaching kids. On the contrary – youth coaches need to apply some degree of discipline in order to maximize the fun and enjoyment of the kids. Youth coaches only have 60-90 minutes to work with kids at practice each week, so they must maintain control and dictate the pace and direction of nearly every minute. Left unsupervised, a group of kids would quickly lose focus and little dictatorships would develop (think: <u>Lord of the Flies</u>). Coaches would not be needed if the kids could coach themselves.

Youth coaches need to be firm with kids to keep them on track and to keep them working as a team. Being firm does not imply being mean or strict. It means being persistent and often insistent on the kids behaving appropriately. Discipline is required when: kids do not listen, kids do not hustle, kids are disrespectful, kids display poor sportsmanship, kids use foul language or, kids intentionally try to hurt someone. Such poor behavior must be dealt with swiftly and in a consistent manner – no double standards. The earlier poor behavior is dealt with, the less it will occur throughout the season. Lighter doses of discipline should be used with the youngest of kids as they are just beginning to learn how to participate in sports and how to compete.

Kids know when coaches are not confident and not truly in control, and they will push the limits of authority for any coach who shows weakness or a lack of discipline. Once a youth coach loses the respect of the kids it is very difficult to regain it and this will usually lead to very ineffective and often negative practices. Take firm control from the beginning and do not relinquish it.

The standard disciplinary tools are running laps and doing pushups/sit ups. Kids that display extremely bad behavior should be made to sit on the sidelines during practice or on the bench during games. The standard disciplinary actions usually work if applied appropriately, but you may need to be creative to get through to some kids. For example, if a player is goofing off during a rebounding drill, separate them from the team and have them throw a ball high off the wall and rebound it several times. Have them continue this until they correct their behavior. This allows the rest of the team to continue without being disrupted and provides the disruptive player with a concentrated dose of practice on an important skill.

In extreme cases, it may be necessary to meet with the parents of a kid that is displaying very little interest in participating in the sport through their severe lack of effort. Let the parents know that you don't want to force the child to play and that the lack of effort may result in a loss of playing time. Kids that have no interest in being on the court, should not be on the court. It is not the coaches job to force a sport on kids or to make kids like a sport. A parent meeting may also be required for kids that exhibit extremely poor behavior. Let parents know that the continued poor behavior will be dealt with using the same corrective actions which will take the child out of the normal flow of practice and may result in a loss of playing time.

The worst youth coaches tend to yell at or threaten kids during times of failure or as a means to motivate. They sometimes take it a step further and physically threaten or harm kids. These tactics may yield short-term results, but their effectiveness cannot be sustained and the long-term damage to kids does not justify their use in youth sports. Fear does not motivate kids into doing what they want to do; it scares them into doing what you want them to do. You must resist the occasional temptation to say or do harmful things to kids if you become upset or frustrated. Continuously remind yourself that they are young kids that are simply playing a game.

2. <u>MISTAKES</u>

Mistakes will happen – a lot. Youth coaches must try not to express any negativity through their comments or actions. Negative body language or facial expressions can do just as much harm as negative comments. Nothing kills a child's joy of sports faster than negative criticism. Use instructive criticism instead to turn mistakes and disappointments into learning opportunities, and make sure your criticism is accompanied with a large dose of praise for their efforts to improve. Remember, mistakes are necessary for growth. They are an indication that the child is pushing themselves to improve.

Mistakes are either honest or behavioral. Honest mistakes are those that are made when a child goes beyond the limit of their capabilities. Kids should never be punished for such mistakes as this will reduce their enjoyment, increase their fear of failure, and eventually lead to a decline in their performance. Kids should be praised for their effort and provided with instructions on how to improve. If you heap on enough praise you can actually disguise your instructive criticism as a compliment. Praise also makes better listeners out of kids which makes them more receptive to instructions.

Behavioral mistakes stem from goofing off, giving little to no effort, or not listening. These mistakes must be dealt with by explaining why the behavior is unacceptable followed by some form of corrective action. If behavioral mistakes are rare for a child, a simple warning may be enough to correct the situation. If such mistakes persist, running laps, doing push-ups, or even imposing a "time out" may be necessary. It must be explained that disrupting practice through poor behavior is unacceptable and will result in additional discipline. Always direct your comments toward the behavior not the individual – it is not personal. Criticism should never be accusatory or demeaning.

3. <u>WINNING & LOSING</u>

Wins and losses should be acknowledged but should not be the primary measure of success. It is important for kids to learn that winning does not make you a winner and losing does not make you a loser. Winners are those that win with humility and lose with dignity. Winners are those that display good sportsmanship at all times and give their best effort. Winners care more about how they compete than if they win or lose.

Wanting to win and trying to win are perfectly normal and healthy attitudes when competing. They're instinctive. But remember, winning is not in the top five reasons why young kids participate in sports to begin with. Unfortunately, through their words and actions, youth coaches (and parents) often make winning the top priority in youth sports. Their expectation of winning and their use of this as the measurement of success are not healthy or productive. Adults also look at winning on an individual performance basis and set impossibly high standards of flawless performance on the kids – where mistakes are unacceptable. These expectations of winning and performing flawlessly are at the root of all that is negative in youth sports.

When kids ask you "who won?" ask them if they had fun, or if they learned anything new, or if they felt good about how they played. When they answer "yes", tell them they won on that basis not on the basis of the score. You will show them that winning is not the focus and that you are more concerned about their level of enjoyment and development as a player. Also remember -- winning is not so important that youth coaches should cheat, bend the rules, treat kids unfairly, or do anything considered to be unethical. They should not encourage their players to hurt the opponent, nor should they play their best players at the expense of the less skilled players.

Losing in sports is unavoidable and it is also the time at which the character of the coaches and players is most clearly revealed. Youth coaches need to maintain a healthy perspective of the game and remain positive and poised through the most difficult times. As a youth coach, the kids on your team will look to you for confidence and reassurance immediately after losses. Regardless of your personal feelings, you cannot show any negative emotions (anger, frustration, etc.). Be especially careful of your facial expressions and body language as these are often stronger displays of emotions than words.

It is perfectly natural for kids to be disappointed and even cry after losing. It shows that they have a passion for the sport and respect for the game. These are the times that kids need support and encouragement the most to help prevent them from being totally demoralized. Regardless of the outcome, always find the positives from the achievements during competitions and enthusiastically praise your players. This will lessen the sting of losses and teach humility after wins. Kids will also have less fear of losing and will enjoy games more. This will typically lead to better performances because the kids will be under much less stress.

Kids that constantly cry or show immense disappointment after losses or mistakes, are under too much pressure. Such stress is not natural for young kids, but it is becoming increasingly prevalent. Unfortunately, the pressure to win usually comes from the parents. Youth coaches can offer subtle advice and suggestions to try and guide parents in the direction of being more supportive and less overbearing, but unless a parent is being especially abusive, youth coaches should not interfere with the parent-child relationship. By following the principles of this guidebook, youth coaches will avoid being the source of stress. They can set a good example by maintaining a positive attitude and taking the focus off of winning and mistakes.

Losses should never be trivialized or treated as totally meaningless. This devalues the game and mitigates the spirit of competition that is vital to all sports. Coaches and players should learn from every game, but losses offer the best learning opportunities as they reveal the weaknesses of the team and the strengths of the opponent. Losses should motivate coaches and players to learn, play harder, and work better as a team. Losses help kids to better appreciate winning.

6. UNDERSTANDING KIDS

Youth coaches must have a basic understanding of how kids think and develop. This will enable them to focus on the needs of the kids. Kids need to feel wanted and valued. Kids need to be surrounded by adults that model positive, poised, and confident behavior. Kids need clear and simple goals that are attainable and unrelated to winning. Kids need tremendous amounts of praise and encouragement. Kids need one instructional voice. Kids need to be treated fairly and with respect.

EARLY BLOOMERS VS. LATE BLOOMERS

Kids learn, grow and develop at different rates. Unfortunately, adults unfairly overestimate or underestimate a child's potential talent based on their performance as youngsters. They make the critical mistake of assuming that talent and ability develop in a predictable trajectory that is set in stone at an early age. Nothing could be further from the truth. Research shows that the performance level of a child under the age of 10 is not an accurate predictor of their performance level as a teenager or adult. Therefore, that 2nd grader that appears to be far superior to the other kids is most likely an early bloomer who will eventually fall back into the pack with the others.

Unfortunately, late bloomers are usually discouraged from participating in sports and lack the support and self-confidence necessary to get more involved. Youth coaches must be the champions for the late bloomers, and should not shy away from teaching these kids who need them the most . This is critical in today's world of youth sports where parents give up on kids that don't show early promise of athletic skill, and where coaches hand-pick the best players and unfairly shun kids that don't perform as well as others.

The cardinal sin of any youth coach is to take away a child's desire to play sports, while their crowning achievement is to motivate and encourage all kids to continue to play sports. That is the mark of a truly great youth coach. Remember, for every young prodigy like Tiger Woods, there are ten late bloomers beating the odds and reaching athletic heights unimaginable when they were 7 or 8 years old. Even the great Michael Jordan didn't make his high school varsity team in his first attempt.

It is very difficult (and often harmful) to accelerate the normal athletic development of a child. We need to realize that kid's bodies are undergoing a complex interaction of physical, mental, and chemical changes that develop on unique timelines. This volatile growth process does not respond well to undue stress applied by overanxious adults. Good youth coaches strive to patiently draw these talents out, while poor coaches carelessly attempt to yank them out.

COMMUNICATION

How and when youth coaches communicate with their kids will determine their success. In fact, **communication is the key to success**. A youth coach may know everything there is to know about sports, but if they cannot communicate their knowledge in a positive manner and with genuine passion and enthusiasm, they will fail as a coach. They will fail to connect with their players and fail to motivate them. Their communication must be overwhelmingly positive, enthusiastic, and continuous.

Positive communication is easy, almost effortless, when things are going well. However, when things are not going well and the team is making numerous mistakes or losing badly to another team, positive communication becomes very difficult. The response to adversity separates good youth coaches from the poor ones. Good youth coaches smile through adversity and maintain a positive attitude. Good youth coaches understand that kids need encouragement the most during tough times and they work hard to interact with the kids and keep their spirits high. Good youth coaches don't brood, show frustration, remain silent, or angrily lash out at kids during periods of adversity.

Youth coaches must continuously praise and encourage their players before, during, and after games and practices. However, they should not praise them for winning. They should praise them for their genuine effort, hustle, perseverance, determination, discipline, team work, competitive spirit, self-control, courage, good sportsmanship, or any number of other positive accomplishments during their play. They must do this regardless of the outcome of competitions. If this is done with positive energy, the sting of losses will be greatly reduced and success will be equated with a positive aspect of their play – not with the scoreboard.

Criticism is unavoidable and should be dealt with using a light touch. The amount of criticism you communicate and the volume level at which it is communicated should pale in comparison to the amount and volume level of your praise and encouragement. Good youth coaches can communicate corrective instructions without creating negative emotions – they do not show anger, frustration or disappointment.

When talking directly to kids, always try to get down on one knee and look them in the eyes to avoid an overbearing presence. They will feel much more comfortable and they will listen better to what you are saying. Humor is also a very effective communication tool when working with kids. It can ease the pain of disappointments, bring some of the more timid kids out of their shells, energize kids, and get kids attention. Humor simply makes kids feel good. Use it early and often.

TEAMWORK

Teamwork is one of the last skills that kids develop – especially in basketball. Kids are too busy improving their individual skills to focus on teammates. Kids also tend to be selfish in general as they are still in the "me" stage of life. Teamwork cannot be forced on kids. It develops over time as a byproduct of the kids going through the same experiences during practice and games. Youth coaches must simply create a positive environment in which camaraderie and trust are encouraged. The "Star Chart" (pg. 71) is also a very helpful tool in improving teamwork. It rewards kids for such selfless activities like hustle, passing, rebounding, setting picks, and defense.

PARENT COACHES

85-90% of youth coaches are parents of one of the players. It is important to separate your role as a parent from that of a coach. You must stop coaching as soon as you leave the gym, and become the loving and supportive parent kids need. Problems occur when you try to assume both roles at once. While away from the gym, only offer coaching advice to your child when they specifically ask for it.

The biggest mistake a parent coach (or parents in general) can make is to continue to coach or to criticize their child on the ride home right after a loss or a poor performance. Make it a rule not to talk about disappointing games or practices, and not to give any advice for at least two hours after they are over. Give kids time to decompress and work things out on their own. They will come to you when they are ready, and that is when you can give them the unconditional love, support, and encouragement they expect from you.

Parent coaches must avoid giving their own child any form of preferential treatment – more playing time, more praise or attention, honorary team captain, etc. Such treatment is a mark of a poor coach with selfish motives. Parent coaches must also avoid being tougher or more demanding on their child. They must treat their own kids fairly or they risk causing major problems in the parent-child relationship. Coaching your own child should be a very special experience that enables a closer bond to be developed.

7. WORKING WITH PARENTS

The key to working with parents is constant communication. Communicate your goals and expectations at the beginning of the season. Communicate the team's progress each week. Communicate to remind parents of game times and locations. Communicate periodically to give them your assessment of the team and any adjustments you may make. Communicate, communicate, communicate! Parents are your allies. Keep them informed so they feel like a member of the team.

As soon as you get your final team roster, call each family just to introduce yourself, let them know a little bit about how you coach, and ask if they have any questions. Just prior to or during the first practice, meet with the parents to discuss your approach to the game, your specific goals for the team, and your expectations of them and the kids. Some of the things you need to communicate at the meeting are as follows:

- Tell them a little about yourself and why you decided to coach.
- Discuss your basic coaching philosophy which should include the "Three Mandatory Elements of Coaching Kids" (pg. 4). Discuss the merits of the positive approach to coaching as outlined in this guidebook.
- Discuss the need for discipline and what your guidelines are for applying it. Let parents know that disciplinary actions are only enforced in response to poor behavior or poor effort, and will include laps, pushups or "timeouts". Let them know that it doesn't include verbally or physically harming the kids, nor does it include embarrassing or demeaning the kids.
- Discuss your goals for the players and team: Improved Skills, Improved Effort, Improved Teamwork, and Improved Sportsmanship. Explain why winning is not one of the main goals.
- Explain the "Star Chart" and explain how it will help achieve the goals.
- Discuss your expectations of the kids: Listen, Hustle, Good Sportsmanship, and Have Fun.
- Discuss your expectations of the parents. Let them know that you expect them to display good sportsmanship at all times and to simply support and encourage the kids from the sidelines. Ask them not to say negative things about the officials or the other team. Ask them not to shout criticisms or bark instructions at the players. Let them know that the game belongs to the kids and what the kids want most is for the parents to simply enjoy watching them play and to root for them.

- Discuss your approach to practice. Let them know that in addition to focusing on the kid's enjoyment, you will be focusing on fundamental basketball skills with an emphasis on dribbling and hustle.
- Discuss your approach to games. Let parents know that you will give the kids equal playing time and that there are no assigned positions. Everyone will be given an opportunity to bring the ball up the court and be the focal point of the offense.
- Discuss the leagues "Code of Conduct" for parents.
- Let the parents know that all feedback is welcome at all times.
- Ask parents to privately communicate any physical or emotional issues that you need to be aware of.
- Go over the required equipment for the kids.
- Go over some of the basic regulations that are specific to your league (ball size, goal height, game length, stealing, etc.).
- Go over how uniforms will be handled.
- Go over the schedule for practice and games. Ask the parents to get the kids to both on time (10-15 minutes early for games).
- Go over the policy for inclement weather.
- Go over the details for team pictures if applicable.
- Discuss extra activities such as post game drinks/snacks, and the post season party for the kids. You can ask for volunteers to organize these functions or you can choose to do it yourself (plan to do it yourself).
- Ask if they have any questions or concerns.

Your initial meeting with the parents will lay the foundation for what you expect from them and what they can expect from you throughout the season. Welcome any feedback they may have regarding your policies or practices throughout the season. This will give them the opportunity to voice any concerns they may have. Always respond quickly and thoughtfully to all communications from the parents.

Regardless of how positive you remain and how effective you are as a coach, you will always have some parents that are impossible to please. Listen to what they have to say, and respond to them accordingly, but don't allow them to coach you. If they feel strongly enough about how things should be run, they should have stepped up to the plate and volunteered themselves. If any parents are especially abusive, disruptive, or disrespectful to any league participants (players, coaches, or officials), speak to them separately and ask them to comply more closely with the Code of Conduct they agreed to uphold at the beginning of the season. It may be necessary to go to your league administrators to deal with severe cases of poor behavior.

8. PRACTICE & GAMES

PRACTICE

The key to practice is being prepared. You must always organize your thoughts and develop a plan. Youth coaches typically have just 60 minutes a week to practice with the kids. Planning ahead will allow you to manage the time effectively and keep everyone working toward their goals. Get to practice early, take immediate control of the kids activities, and keep everyone on pace. The first practice of the season is especially critical. Refer to Chapter 17 ("The First Practice") for a helpful checklist you can use for your first practice.

Regardless of the age group, youth coaches must focus almost exclusively on the fundamentals of the game. Dribbling – not shooting – is the secret to developing better basketball players and teams. It is by far the most important skill to develop in young kids. The less a kid is able to dribble, the less involved they are in practice and games. Improving their ability to dribble also gives kids a better feel for the ball and their overall ball handling improves. They increase their ability to secure rebounds and catch passes. It is no coincidence that the best youth players are those that are able to dribble well. The "Practice Plans" (pg. 74) in this guidebook focus heavily on ball handling. They were designed specifically to support the basic goals for the team and to support all of the fundamental skills in the "Star Chart".

The "Practice Plans" are also designed for specific age groups. The plans become more advanced as the kids get older. For instance, kids 4-6 usually don't have the strength necessary to shoot the ball with the proper form. Don't worry about teaching them the textbook shooting form at this age. You can wait until they get older and stronger to teach them the proper technique. Tell the youngest kids to get their shooting hand under the ball, bend their legs and then do whatever they can to get the ball in the hoop. Let them enjoy the feeling of simply making shots.

Below are some additional tips on how to conduct successful practice sessions:

- Keep it Safe – Strictly follow the safety measures outlined earlier in the guidebook.
- Keep it Fun – Keep the atmosphere in practices humorous and light by maintaining your positive attitude. The kids will enjoy themselves more and learn more as well.

- Keep it Energetic – Maintain a high level of energy and enthusiasm throughout the entire practice. Get out on the floor and really interact with the kids. They will feed off your energy. Try to minimize long talks with kids. Talking for more than a couple of minutes is boring and zaps their energy and enthusiasm. Kids learn more by doing than by listening to speeches.

- Keep it Moving – Kids get bored and distracted very easily. Keep things moving briskly by changing activities every few minutes and keep the mood light and upbeat. If you have help at practice and enough room, try to split the team into smaller groups. This will allow different drills to be done simultaneously and will allow more drills to be done.

- Keep it Simple – Don't try to teach complex skills or multiple skills at the same time. Break down skills into bite-size pieces so kids can better grasp the concepts. Take things step by step until they are ready to put them all together.

- Keep it in Control – Kids need guidance and supervision to keep them focused. Use appropriate amounts of discipline, time management, and cheerleading to maintain control of the kids and to keep their attention.

- Keep it Fair – Treat kids equally when it comes to praise and discipline. Do not show favor or disfavor to some kids more than others. Do not treat the most skilled players or your own child any differently than other kids. Show all of the kids that they are equally important.

- Keep it Balanced – Try to match up players with similar levels of ability in order to keep things competitive.

- Keep it in Perspective – Don't forget you are working with young kids and not little adults. Don't forget that you are there for the kids and the kids are there to play a game they enjoy. You are there to teach the kids how to play.

GAMES

Games offer the kids a chance to perform for their friends and family. Don't take away from their fun by bickering with the officials or yelling at the team when they make mistakes. Constantly encourage the kids to play hard and hustle and trust them to do their best. When they do make mistakes, encourage them even more to keep their head in the game and to keep trying.

For 1st grade and under, coaches are often allowed to stand on the playing area and provide instructions to the kids. These games are often a comedy of errors as the kids usually run around in a frenzy chasing after the ball. It is nearly impossible to control the activity of the entire team, but you can somewhat control the activity of individual players. By addressing each player individually, you will get their attention and they will be better able to follow instructions. Youth coaches must stay on the sideline for 2nd grade and above games. Regardless of where the coach's communication comes from, it should always be overwhelmingly positive, encouraging, and enthusiastic.

A day or two prior to games, coaches need to spend some time determining the basic playing schedule that will provide a rough outline of which players will start the game, and when players will come in and out of the game. Players can be split into two different squads that will play together during their time in the game. The squads should contain kids with different skill levels. Don't build a squad with the best players and another with the least skilled players. This will create an imbalance and it may lead to some embarrassing moments for some of the kids. Put some thought into who will play together and how the squads will be rotated. It is recommended that a simple spreadsheet be created to document the playing time for each game. This will help ensure you are giving each player a fair amount of playing time. Don't take this exercise lightly – especially if you have an odd number of players or more than 10 players.

All youth coaches are tempted to keep their best players in for the majority of games or designate the best players as the primary ball handlers in order to give them the best chance to win. By doing this, youth coaches are devaluing the less skilled players and treating them unfairly in order to satisfy their personal desire to win and avoid the perceived embarrassment and loss of respect as a coach. These motivations are selfish and the kid's wants and needs are not the main consideration. This is the heart of the problem in youth sports today. The adults want to win, but the kids just want to play. It's their game – let them play! Let all of the kids experience being the focal point of the offense. This is critical to their development.

During games have the kids take turns bringing the ball down the court – playing point guard. It is best to designate 2-4 players as point guards for each game and then rotate the players throughout the season to give them all a chance to play this important position. Tell the players about this strategy ahead of time so they will understand what you are doing. You will be amazed at how much confidence kids gain simply by being given the opportunity to dribble the ball up the court. Even the less skilled ball handlers will often surprise you on how well they do. Yes – they will make mistakes, but that's part of the learning process and it's necessary for growth.

Never yell at the officials and never use fowl or accusatory language. Always try to approach them in a calm manner during a break in the game and be as positive as possible. This will be the hardest thing you have to do during games and it will take all of the discipline you have not to let your frustrations show. Remember that most of the officials are inexperienced and they will make mistakes. Try to let their mistakes go without comment unless there seems to be a misunderstanding of the rules. At that point ask them to clarify the rules so everyone is on the same page. Also, try not to let poor behavior or poor sportsmanship by the other coach or players impact your behavior or attitude. Rise above the situation and remember that all of the kids are watching you.

Here are a few coaching tips for game day:
- Get to the game site early.
- Once the court is available, have the players warm up by doing one or two layup or shooting drills – do not allow the players to just shoot around haphazardly.
- Keep the players loose and upbeat by joking around with them and giving them quick pep talks on an individual basis.
- During warm-ups, select a team captain for the game. Select a different player for each game.
- Also during warm-ups, let the players know who will be starting the game. Every player should be given an equal number of opportunities to start games throughout the season.
- Keep an eye on the opposing team during warm-ups to identify their more skilled players. Make sure you have your better defenders matched up with those players.
- A few minutes before the game begins, huddle the team together and go over the game plan and remind them how the offense should be run. Don't overload them with instructions.
- Communicate to the players throughout the game and give them plenty of enthusiastic praise and instructions.
- Push your players to hustle at all times by going after loose balls and rebounds.
- Stay positive when communicating with players, officials, coaches, and parents. Games can get emotional so try to remain calm and always set a good example for the kids.
- When things are not going well, stay calm and composed. Smile at the players, maintain a reassuring tone, and then give them specific instructions on how to turn things around.
- It's okay to be loud, just don't shout or yell at the players.
- Do not allow the players to leave the bench unless they need to use the restroom or get some water.

- Encourage the players on the bench to pay attention to the game and cheer on their teammates – do not allow them to cheer against the opponent.
- Immediately address any moments of poor sportsmanship by your players. Call a time out if necessary to address the team. Depending on the severity of the actions, players may need to be removed from the game.
- Keep track of playing time to ensure relatively equal playing time.
- Make sure the players lineup of for a post-game handshake with the opposing team.
- After the handshake, huddle the team and let them know what they did that was positive, and have them do a final team cheer.

PART 2: OFFENSE

A good offense in basketball is all about proper spacing. The objective of players on offense is to score, but in order to do this effectively they must first create space between themselves and the defense. The offense must get a shooter in an open area in order to attempt a good shot – the closer the area is to the basket the more likelihood of success. Therefore, until a shot can be taken, everything an offensive player does should be with the intent of getting to an open area of the court or helping a teammate get to an open area of the court. Remind kids of this fundamental aspect of the game throughout the season. This is rarely explained to young players.

Young kids all want the ball and they all want to shoot. Whoever has the ball will usually be quickly surrounded by their teammates all asking for the ball. Besides the offensive players being crowded into a small area, this also brings all of the defensive players into the same area. The younger the kids are, the more this will happen. Before you roll out the basketballs and have the kids dribble, pass, and shoot, teach them the "Basic Offensive Moves" in the next chapter that every player needs to know to create space on offense. It won't immediately stop them from crowding around the ball, but they will eventually learn to move further and further away.

The cause of congested offenses is often due to kid's inability to maintain their dribble. Kids often stop dribbling soon after they cross the half court line or when the defense gets close to them. As soon as this happens the other offensive players will swarm all around the ball to "help" their teammate. This is another reason why dribbling is the most important skill to develop in kids. It makes the game much easier for young kids, and it helps to minimize the spacing issues.

9. BASIC OFFENSIVE MOVES

Jab Step & Cutting

The jab step is deceptive move in which a player firmly and quickly jabs (or stomps) one of their feet in one direction with their upper body also leaning in that direction, and then immediately moves (cuts) in the opposite direction. The intent is to make the defense think you are going in one direction when your goal is to go in the opposite direction – thereby creating space between yourself and the defender. This move is most often used by offensive players that do not have the ball and are attempting to get open to receive a pass or are trying to set a pick for a teammate. Dribblers can also use this move in conjunction with a "Crossover Dribble". Prior to moving anywhere on the court, offensive players should almost always fake with a "Jab Step" to keep the defense off balance.

Cutting is when a player makes a sudden move in a certain direction in order to create space or to get to a spot on the court before the defense can catch up. When a player makes a jab step and then moves in the opposite direction, that move is called a cut. Players usually employ a jab step before making a cut, but cuts can be made from a stationary position where the unexpected move surprises the defense.

Kids under 8 years old may not have much trouble performing these moves, but they will have an extremely hard time remembering to perform them during game situations. As a coach, you must just continue to remind them to try to make these moves whenever possible. You will be setting the proper foundation for these basic offensive moves to eventually take hold in their minds.

Jump Stop or Quick Stop

This is a basic move that is intended to allow players to maintain control of their bodies as they come to a complete stop. It can be performed by defensive and offensive players. The move is performed by a player that is running. As the player approaches the point where they want to stop, they 1) slow their momentum, 2) jump slightly into the air, 3) plant both feet firmly on the floor just wider than shoulder width, 4) bend their knees, and 5) put their hands up with their elbows bent (unless they are dribbling). The player's momentum should not carry them past the point of the stop.

Pivots

The pivot is a fundamental move by offensive players. It is done to allow players to maintain possession of the ball without traveling. In simple terms, the move is performed by turning in any direction while keeping one foot on the floor in the same spot. When pivoting with the ball, players should firmly hold the ball with both hands with their elbows pointing out. This allows for better protection from defenders.

In order to pivot players must spin (or pivot) on the balls of their feet. Once a player with the ball has established a pivot foot they cannot switch to the other foot. Players almost always establish their off foot (the foot opposite their shooting hand) as the pivot foot. Pivoting is critical because it allows players to 1) avoid defenders, 2) get in a better position to make a pass, 3) jab step and fake defenders, and 4) get in better position to drive past defenders.

Pivots can also be done by offensive players that don't have the ball where the move can be used to spin around or away from defenders in order to get open to receive a pass. When players pivot without the ball, they should have their hands in the air with their elbows bent. This allows the player to take up more space and keep defenders away.

Fakes

The purpose of "Fakes" is to deceive the defense and throw them off balance. They can be performed with or without the ball. The "Jab Step" is a prime example of a fake without the ball. Faking shots, passes, and dribble moves involves quickly moving the ball in one direction in an attempt to make the defense commit to a movement or to make them hesitate long enough to clear space. The head, shoulders and arms can also be moved along with the ball to make the fake much more effective.

Faking is not a difficult concept for kids to grasp but it is something they hardly ever do. They simply do not think about it during the frenzy of game situations. You can introduce younger players to fakes and explain the purpose, but don't expect them to use them that often. As players get more experienced and the game slows down for them, they will learn to use fakes more often.

Triple Threat Position

This is a fundamental position that will take most kids a great deal of time to fully understand and execute. Players must be in the front court within shooting range for the "threat" to be effective. Players can get into this position as soon as they receive a pass. After catching the ball players should:

1) Pivot with their off foot (opposite of their shooting hand) and get squared up to the basket – this will allow them to see the basket, the defense and their teammates. 2) Bend their knees and slightly lean forward with their pivot foot in front of the other foot -- most of their weight should be on the pivot foot so they can be ready to push off the pivot foot at any second. 3) Place their hands on the ball in the shooting position and hold the ball back and away from the defense at the midsection of their body on the shooting side.

At this point the player is a threat to the defense in three ways – they can dribble the ball, pass the ball, or shoot the ball. Fakes are extremely effective in this position since the defense has to be prepared to guard all three threats. If a player receives the ball and immediately starts to dribble, they can no longer get into the triple threat position. The worst thing a player can do is stop their dribble without a passing or shooting opportunity. This takes away the primary dribbling threat and will allow the defense to smother the passing and shooting options of the offensive player. The "Triple Threat" position forces defenses to back off the offensive player to be in a better position to stop them from dribbling to the basket.

Posting or Posting Up

This is a fundamental move used by offensive players to position their bodies in front of a defender in order to get open for a pass. This move is traditionally performed by players on the low and high posts around the basket. This is why it is referred to as "posting" or "posting up" the defense. However, posting can be done anywhere on the court and it is especially effective during inbound plays. Instead of just running to the ball and yelling for a pass with the defender standing next to them, have kids on offense try to use a simple post position when they want to get open for a pass. This can reduce congestion around the ball and make passing easier.

When a player is in a posting position they have the defender directly behind them; they have their feet wide and their knees slightly bent; they have their arms up and bent at the elbows; they have their hands open as targets for a pass; and they are slightly bent at the waist with their backside in contact with the defender. The defense will usually attempt to get in front of the post player. Therefore, the post player must continue to move (slide) their feet and keep their body in front and in contact with the defender. This is exactly like boxing out during a rebound. The post player must match the aggressiveness of the defender and really push back with their lower body. The arms can be used to some degree to keep the defender in back, but aggressive use of the arms will result in an offensive foul.

If the offensive player starts out in front of the defender, they just need to maintain their post position. If the offensive player starts out behind the defender, they must make a quick and aggressive move to get in front. Such moves normally start with getting one foot in front of the defender and then using the rest of the body as leverage to wedge in front. A quick spin move (pivot) around the defender is a more advanced move that can be used. Players must be careful not to use their arms too much and must be especially careful not to use their hands as this will lead to fouls.

Setting Picks or Screens

Setting picks is another fundamental move for any offense. Younger kids will struggle with how and when to set picks, but keep working on it with them as it will provide them with a solid foundation as they get more experienced. Second and third grade is typically when setting picks becomes more common. Setting picks involves simply blocking the path of a defender to allow a teammate to get open for a pass, shot, or drive to the basket. It is performed by the offensive player quickly moving into position on either side of (side pick) or directly behind (back pick) a defensive player. The player setting the pick must keep both feet firmly on the floor at shoulder width, and have their arms firmly pressed against their sides. Their knees should be slightly bent and their hands should be together in front of their bodies. This will help them brace for a solid bump from the defender – they must remain solidly in place and not give any ground to the defender.

It is important for the player setting the pick to avoid fouling by not leaning too far forward or sideways; not sticking out their arms, elbows, legs or feet to block the defender and; not using their hands to grab a defender. It is also important for the offensive player that the pick is being set for not to move too soon toward the picking player, and to get as close as possible to the picking player to keep the defender from squeezing through the pick. The two offensive players should actually slightly brush their shoulders together. Coordinating the moves between the two offensive players will be the toughest part to learn. Jab steps by both offensive players make picks extremely effective – especially by the player being picked as they can "set up" their defender and put them in a position to make the pick very effective.

The offensive player that the pick is being set for should almost always move in the direction of the pick. The only exception is when their defender "cheats" the pick by moving far to the side of the pick before the pick is actually set – they are moving to the spot they expect their player to move to. When this happens the player that the pick is being set for may have a clear path to the basket and should immediately drive to the basket – away from the pick. If they have the ball, they can take it in for a layup. If they don't have the ball they will be open for a pass as they move to the basket. Kids will always try to "cheat" on defense. Teach your kids to always take advantage of these situations since they usually create a scenario in which the offensive player is left undefended with a clear path to the basket.

Pick & Roll

This is a classic offensive move. It is performed by an offensive player that sets a pick for a teammate with the ball. Once the pick is set, the player with the ball dribbles past the picker. The picker then pivots toward the basket (rolls) in the same direction of the dribbler, and quickly moves to the basket with their hands up and ready to receive a pass. By rolling to the basket, the picker puts the picked defender behind them and creates space as they move to the basket. Other defenders must help to prevent the roller from getting an open shot.

10. FUNDAMENTAL SKILLS

Ball Handling

Ball handling is usually associated with dribbling. However, ball handling in its simplest form is all about getting a feel for the ball so that the fingers and hands gain a tactile memory of the texture and weight of the ball. Dribbling is certainly a form of ball handling, but it is important enough to have its own category.

Young kids need to learn more basic ball handling moves that will enable their hands to get stronger and their fingers to get more flexible. They develop a feel for the ball that will enable them to confidently grasp the ball in any situation. The ball handling drills outlined in this book are perfect to give kids as homework assignments. They don't require a basket, they can be done with almost any type of ball, and they can be done indoors when the weather is bad.

Dribbling

Have kids dribble as soon as they get in the gym. Make them dribble early and often, and then make them dribble some more. Dribbling is by far the most important skill to develop in young players. It will allow them to evade or elude the defense and advance the ball to the basket or to an open area of the court. The simple act of bouncing the ball off the floor while maintaining control is what should be taught to pre-schoolers and most 1st graders. Focus on developing their dribbling with their strong hand, but have them spend some time using their weak hand as well. 1st and 2nd grade is when kids should begin dribbling faster, changing directions while dribbling, and using their weak hand more often.

It is also very important that the kids do not stop dribbling until they have an open shot or can make a good pass. Kids that stop dribbling too soon will be swarmed by their teammates – and all of the defenders. Many youth leagues don't allow defenses to steal the ball from a dribbler until the 3rd grade (stealing passes is usually allowed for all grade levels). Remind the kids of this so they will not be afraid when the defense gets near them and they will not stop dribbling. Fear is what makes most kids stop dribbling.

Since stealing from dribblers is usually allowed in 3rd grade and above, ball protection should be heavily stressed to kids at this age. The youth coach should emphasize keeping the ball low with the off-hand up and out to shield the ball from defenders. Kids should also learn how to dribble with their backs to the defender to make it hard for the defense to get to the ball. The use of their weak hand and faster movements should also be stressed as it will allow them to quickly move in any direction without losing control of the ball. Once the essential elements of controlling the dribble and protecting the ball are mastered, kids can move forward and learn the more advanced dribbling techniques outlined in the "Dribbling Drills" section (pg. 40) of this guidebook.

By focusing on developing dribbling skills in practice, kids will get better by the end of the season. However, don't expect huge improvements unless the kids practice on their own as well. Ask kids to do some of the basic drills at home for at least 10 minutes a day – give them one of the dribble or ball handling drills as a simple homework assignment. Even if they spend time dribbling a rubber ball in the basement, they will make great progress if they consistently practice the basic motion away from the gym.

These basic mechanics need to be maintained whenever players are dribbling:
- Dribble with one hand at a time.
- Keep the hand on top of the ball.
- Use the fingers/fingertips not the palm of the hand.
- Press or push the ball down; don't slap it.
- Slightly bend the knees.
- Slightly bend at the waist.
- Maintain good balance with the feet spread apart.
- Don't bounce the ball too high (keep it below the waist, ideally around the knees).
- Keep the off hand/arm up and in front to protect the ball from defenders.
- Keep your head up and eyes forward so you can see the basket, your teammates, and the defense.
- Once you start, don't stop dribbling until you can pass or shoot.
- Turn your back to the defender when being closely guarded to protect the ball.

Passing
Basketball, at its core, is a team sport, and passing is an essential element of teamwork. Passing is a skill that can be very difficult for young kids to develop. While there are always exceptions, kids in 1st grade and below will struggle a great deal with passing – especially with catching passes. They will be able to go through the basic passing drills during practice, but they will

likely struggle to make good passes during game situations. Youth coaches must remain patient and keep using the passing drills to improve their skills.

Kids in 2nd and 3rd grade will be much better at passing and catching while stationary, but will struggle when performing these skills while moving. This is normal for kids at this age because their hand eye coordination has yet to develop the ability to judge targets moving in different directions. Once again, be patient as their passing performance during practice will almost always exceed their performance during real games.

Another thing that makes passing very difficult is the lack of proper spacing by kids during game situations. Kids on offense, especially the youngest ones, will tend to crowd around whoever has the ball yelling "pass it...pass it!" This herd mentality is prevalent for most kids under 10 years old, and it will take a great deal of patience and persistence to break them of this habit. Utilize the "Passing Drills" (pg. 44) to teach floor spacing and to get kids used to moving to open areas of the court. The "4-Corners" (pg. 44) drill is an especially effective tool for teaching floor spacing.

These basic mechanics need to be maintained whenever players are passing:
- Always pass with at least one foot (preferably two) on the floor.
- Palms facing in while holding the ball before the pass with thumbs up.
- Follow through by fully extending the arms, hands, and fingers at the end of the pass with the palms facing out and thumbs down.
- Always pass away from the defender.
- Always look at the player you are passing to and make sure they are looking at you.
- Always step toward the player you are passing to – step into the pass.
- If passing to a running teammate, always lead them by passing in front of them.
- Use fake passes whenever possible – especially when being closely guarded.

When Receiving Passes:
- Always come toward the ball when receiving a pass and keep your eyes on it until it has been secured.
- Always use two hands when receiving a pass.
- Always show the passer your hands to give them a target to throw to.
- Unless you are on the run, always try to pivot and face the basket after receiving a pass ("Triple Threat" position).

- Don't automatically start dribbling as soon as you get the ball. Most young kids take one or two dribbles as soon as they get the ball and then stop – this is one of the worst thing they can do on offense.

Shooting

The textbook shooting form and motion is described below. However, almost all kids less than 7 years old and many under 10, will not be able to use the proper form simply because they are not strong enough or have not been taught the correct form. These kids will start with the ball anywhere from the thighs to the stomach and use their entire bodies to heave the ball to the basket. This is perfectly fine as a starting point. Work with them to get their hands in the proper position and following through, but don't worry too much about the starting position of the ball. In the beginning, kids need to work on simply getting the ball up to the basket in whatever manner works best for them. Don't worry too much about the textbook mechanics mentioned below at this point. You can give kids some exposure to the proper mechanics of a shot, but do not expect them to be able to perform them all until they are 8 or 9 years old – even then, they will not be able to do everything with 100% proper technique.

There are no official statistics, but a conservative estimate is that 80% of the points made in youth leagues are from layups – fast break layups and put back layups from rebounds. Work on the shooting forms, but make sure you spend a good deal of time having the kids practice the layup drills. This has the added benefit of allowing kids to practice dribbling at the same time. As kids get into 2nd and 3rd grade, they will be stronger, better dribblers and have better spacing which will lead to more outside shots.

All kids love to shoot the ball and they get no greater thrill than having the ball go in the basket. Left unsupervised, kids of all ages will immediately start shooting from as far away as possible. Do not let them do this during practice or games and encourage them not to do this when away from the gym. They need to work on realistic shots. A good rule of thumb is to have the kids shoot no further than twice their age in feet from the basket. So, if a kid is 7 years old, their maximum range should be about 14 feet from the basket. Doing the shooting drills outlined in this guidebook will help the players shoot better, but you will still run into several kids that experience at least one of the following problems:

Problem 1: Kids can't get the ball up to the rim.
- This is typically a problem for kids 7 years old and under.

- Have the kids hold the ball with both hands -- with their shooting hand under the ball and their off hand on the side of the ball. Then have them "cock" the ball down and as far back as possible.
- Have the kids really bend their knees and then thrust the ball up with as much force as possible. Tell the kids to aim for the top of the backboard and really follow through.
- Make adjustments to the force of the shot or the position of the hands and body until the kids are consistently making or coming close to making shots. The kids can also practice their shooting against a wall where they try to shoot the ball high off the wall – the goal is to make them stronger and comfortable with the motion.
- During shooting drills have these kids keep shooting these types of shots until they are too fatigued to get it close to the rim. This will actually help them grow stronger and within 3 to 4 practices they should have little trouble getting the ball above the rim. The process will be greatly expedited if the kids also do these exercises at home.

Problem 2: Kids shoot the ball too hard and with very little touch.
- This is often caused by kids always heaving the ball from long distances and never getting a feel for shooting.
- Have the kids stand about half way between the foul line and the basket and have them attempt to shoot the ball into the basket.
- While they do this, pay close attention to their form. Especially watch how the ball is coming off the hand. The ball may not be rolling off of the fingers; it may be releasing right off of the palm in a "shot put" manner. They may also be extending the arm too fast in a jerky motion – like snapping a rubber band.
- These kids need to develop a better feel for the shooting motion. Have them work a few extra minutes on the "Form Shooting" and "Back Spin" drills outlined later (pg. 46).
- When you are ready to have these kids shoot at the basket, have them start close and then work their way out. Begin by having them stand just a couple of feet away from the basket at an angle near the lower block of the free throw lane. Have them attempt to shoot the ball off the backboard and into the basket. Have them go to different locations around the basket and start to work your way out as they get more comfortable and accurate from each distance.

Problem 3: Kids shoot the ball way to the right or left of the basket.

- This problem is almost always related to the position of the hands and the elbow. In most cases, the kids are shooting with both hands on the sides of the ball and neither hand is aiming directly at the basket.

- Have the kids perform a couple of free throws and watch their form closely. Make sure they are not shooting with both hands and make sure their shooting hand is positioned properly beneath and behind the middle of the ball and is pointing at the basket during the follow through. Make sure their off hand is not touching the ball as the ball is moving toward the basket. Make sure their shooting elbow is not flared outward or inward too much (more than 45 degrees). Also make sure that they are taking their time and looking at the basket before shooting.

- These kids need to develop better shooting forms. Have them work a few extra minutes on the "Form Shooting" and "Back Spin" drills outlined below (pg. 46).

- As these kids work on changing their shooting form, they may lose some distance on their shot until they get used to shooting properly. Have them work close to the basket at first and then have them work their way out from the basket as they get more comfortable.

Shooting Mechanics

Shooting involves two parts – holding the ball and then going through the motion of actually shooting the ball.

Holding the ball:

1. The ball should be held just above shoulder height on the same side of the head as the shooting hand.
2. The arm of the shooting hand should be bent with the elbow even with the armpit and the hand just above the shoulder with the palm of the hand facing up. The ball can then be placed on the palm and heel of the shooting hand with the fingers supporting the back of the ball.
3. The fingers should not be too close or too far apart. One way to ensure proper finger separation is to have the kids spread their fingers apart as far as they can and then relax the hand. At the point the hand relaxes, the fingers will be separated properly.
4. The thumb and index finger of the shooting hand should loosely form an "L" shape with the index finger close to the middle of the ball.
5. The off-hand should be placed on the side of the ball to offer some support before the shot is taken. As soon as the shooting hand begins

the shooting motion, the off-hand should remain still (should not go with the ball) while the ball is being pushed (shot) to the basket.

Shooting the ball – the "BEEEF" method:

1. **B**alance – The kids should get into an athletic stance with their feet shoulder width apart; the foot on the side of the shooting hand slightly in front of the other foot; knees slightly bent.

2. **E**yes on Target – The kids need to focus on the rim when they are shooting. Looking at the basket may seem like an obvious thing to do, but kids need to be reminded of this as they often shoot quickly before looking. The eyes should remain on the basket even during the flight of the ball.

3. **E**lbow Pointing at Target – The elbow should be bent with the tip pointing at the basket. At this point, you should be able to draw a straight line from the ball through the shooting hand, elbow, knee, and foot. "Squaring Up" to the basket is necessary for the proper elbow position to take place.

4. **E**xtend the Arm – Once the ball is comfortably sitting in the shooting hand with the elbow bent, the arm needs to be extended up and out in order to propel the ball toward the basket. The arm should not move at lightning speed but should accelerate smoothly through the motion in coordination with the legs elevating from their bent position. The shooting arm should be fully extended as the ball is released.

5. **F**ollow Through – As the arm is extended, the ball rolls off of the finger tips of the shooting hand and the wrist and fingers are snapped downward and held in this exaggerated position while the ball is in flight. The wrist and hand should resemble a goose neck. Sticking your hand in a cookie jar is another way to describe the exaggerated position of the hand. A good follow through aids in the height, distance, and accuracy of a shot and helps give the ball a proper backspin.

11. OFFENSIVE DRILLS

Fundamental Movement Drills

Jab/Cut Basic (simple) – Have the kids line up behind each other facing the basket at the foul line. Then have them take a jab step in either direction followed by a cut in the opposite direction where they curl around and go to the back of the line.

Jab/Cut Layup (simple) – Have the kids form one line at the free throw line and another line in the right wing area (facing the basket). A ball is given to the first player at the foul line – this is the passer. The first player on the wing takes a jab step and then makes a quick cut to the basket. The passer makes a bounce pass to the cutter who takes the ball in for a layup and then goes to the end of the passing line. The passer rebounds the ball, gives it to the next passer in line, and then goes to the end of the other line on the wing. If the kids are too young or inexperienced to make decent passes, have all of the kids line up on the wing and you (the coach) can make the passes.

Basic Jump Stop (simple) – Have the kids line up under the basket and run to the foul line one at a time. As they approach the foul line they need to perform a jump stop. Provide corrective instructions as needed.

Jump Stop Pivot (simple) – Have the kids perform the "Basic Jump Stop" as described above, but have the kids pivot around toward the basket as soon as their feet are planted.

Dribble/Jump Stop/Pivot/Pass (moderate) – This drill puts several of the basic moves together. Start by having the kids line up under the basket. The first player dribbles the ball quickly to the foul line, performs a jump stop, pivots back toward the basket, and then passes the ball to the next player in line. This continues until every player has had 3-5 turns.

Triple Threat Yells (moderate) – Have the kids line up at the top of the key. Have the first player run to the foul line as the coach passes them a ball. When they receive the ball they should immediately get into the triple threat position and then yell each of the threats as they demonstrate them. They should jab step as if they will dribble and yell "dribble"; they should fake a shot and yell "shot"; and then they should pass the ball back to the coach and yell "pass". The next player in line comes forward to receive their pass. This reinforces the options that they have.

Posting Up (moderate) – Have the kids form one line anywhere around the basket. The first player will be the offensive player and the second player will be the defensive player – you can do this drill with the offensive player starting in front of the defender or behind them (harder). The coach will stand 10-15 feet away with a ball and make a pass to the offensive player if they are able to establish a post position on the defender for 3-5 seconds. You have the option of allowing the offensive player to make a move to the basket once they receive the ball. When the first two players have gone, the offensive player runs to the end of the line and the defensive player becomes the new offensive player. The next player in line plays defense. Remind the defense not to allow the offensive player to have an open lane to the basket – pass it to the offensive player if the defense leaves them wide open. You can also have a third player make the passes instead of the coach.

Basic Pick (moderate) – Have the kids form two lines – one at the low post just outside of the paint and one at the elbow (high post) of the foul line on the same side as the other line. The high post player is given a ball and dribbles as they go around the picker. The first player in each line should be facing each other. The coach can act as the defender guarding the player at the high post (with their back to the basket). The player on the low post takes a jab step as if they are going under the basket to the other side of the lane, and then they cut up to the high post and set a pick on the defender. The high post player waits for the pick, takes a jab step away from the picker, and brushes by the picker as soon as they have set their feet. Provide corrective instructions to both players to make sure they are executing the move properly. You can set up similar picks in different areas of the court and have kids act as defenders on one or both offensive players.

Basic Pick & Roll Drill (advanced) – Have the kids set up just like the "Basic Pick" drill, but have the picker execute a roll by pivoting toward the basket and putting the defender behind them. The dribbler waits for the pick and then brushes by the picker. The dribbler makes eye contact with the player rolling to the basket and passes them the ball for a layup.

Ball Handling Drills

Ball Toss (simple) – This is a warm up move in which the kids toss the ball from one hand to the next. Their hands should be about 1 foot apart, and they must maintain control of the ball throughout the drill. Have them start out slow and then speed up as much as possible. For older kids, have them try to use their fingertips only.

Ball Spins (simple) – This drill can be done in two different ways. First, have the kids simply spin the ball using both hands where the ball remains in between the hands (the ball should rotate toward the player). Once they are comfortable with this basic move, have the kids spin the ball and throw it a couple of feet into the air at the same time. They need to catch the ball without it hitting the ground.

Wrap Arounds (moderate) – This is a classic drill performed by moving a ball from hand to hand while wrapping it around a body part. The kids can wrap the ball around one leg, both legs, their knees, their waist, and their head – the most advanced version involves moving the ball in a figure eight pattern around and between the legs. It will take time for kids to perform wrap arounds without losing control of the ball, but they will eventually get the hang of it if they start slow and work up to faster speeds – it also helps when their arms grow longer and hands get bigger.

Ball Drops (moderate) – Have the kids hold a ball between their legs – one hand in front of the legs, one hand behind the legs. They need to let the ball bounce once off the floor, switch hands quickly and catch ball before it bounces again.

Figure Eights (advanced) – This is a dribbling drill in which the kids stand with their legs spread out wide while dribbling the ball in a figure eight pattern around and between their legs. The kids start by dribbling the ball in front with one hand and then bouncing the ball between their legs and behind them where the other hand takes control of the ball. The second hand continues to dribble the ball around the outside of their leg (the leg on the same side as the dribbling hand) and toward the front. The ball is then dribbled between the legs again where the first hand takes back control and dribbles around the outside of the other leg toward the front. That is one complete figure eight. The kids should strive to keep the ball low to the ground and to take several short, rapid dribbles instead a few long dribbles.

Machine Gun (advanced) – This is a very difficult dribble drill where the ball is dribbled rapidly with both hands positioned in the front and then the back of the body in an alternating pattern. The ball does not go around the legs as with the figure eight drill – it is dribbled in the same spot between the legs. The players must have their legs spread at shoulder width and squat toward the ground with their backs relatively straight. The drill begins with one hand bouncing the ball once between their legs. Then the second hand quickly dribbles the ball once. While the second hand is making its motion to dribble the ball, the first hand reaches back behind the leg and dribbles the ball right after the second hand is done. The second is rapidly sent back behind the

39

other leg and dribbles the ball once. While this occurs the first hand is moved back to the front where it dribbles once. The second hand quickly moves forward to perform its dribble. That completes one cycle of this move. The hands must move extremely fast (like a machine gun) to perform this movement.

Dribbling Drills

Dribble Laps (simple) – This is a great warm up for the start of any practice. The kids simply dribble while doing laps around the court. Have them start off slow and then work up to a faster pace. Have them use their weak hand for some of the laps as well.

Cone Dribble (simple) – This is also a good warm up drill for practice. Simply set up some cones in a straight line or staggered pattern down the length of the court (or in a square pattern for half court) and have the kids weave around the cones while dribbling. For beginners it is fine for them to keep the ball in their strong hand the entire time, but others need to switch hands ("Crossover Dribble") just after passing each cone. The ball should be dribbled with the hand that is farthest from the cone (as if the cone is a defender). Therefore, a player going around the left side of a cone should be dribbling with their left hand. Once they pass the cone, they should crossover to the right hand as they approach the right side of the next cone….and so on.

More advanced dribblers can incorporate between the legs or spin dribbles as well. This drill is perfect for combining with a layup drill, where the players go around the final cone in a position to drive to the basket for a layup. Once players get to the last cone or shoot a layup, have them dribble quickly to the back of the line, making sure they stay out of the way of the players still navigating through the cones.

Spot Dribble (simple) – This is a stationary dribble where the kids try to hit the same spot on the floor with every bounce. This drill is especially good for kids new to basketball and for those learning how to use their weak hands. This technique allows kids to get a feel for the ball and helps them create some muscle memory. This is also a good warm up drill for better dribblers. They can really pound the ball hard and switch from hand to the other.

V-Dribble (simple) – This is a stationary dribble that is very similar to the "Spot Dribble". It is performed by bouncing the ball on the same spot with the same hand, but with the ball moving from side to side. When you trace the movement of the ball, it forms a "V" with the point being the spot on the floor. Have the kids do this drill with each hand and also have them do the drill going from one hand to the other after each bounce.

Controlled Dribble (simple) – This is the standard dribbling method. Have the kids stand still or slowly walk forward while dribbling with one hand. Yell "change" and have the kids switch to the other hand. Have them switch about 10 times. Make sure the kids have their legs bent and dribble the ball no higher than their knees. You can speed up the pace when the kids get more comfortable.

Speed Dribble (simple) – This dribble is used on fast breaks or for quick transitions down and around the court. Have the kids run as fast as they can while dribbling down the court. Make sure the kids don't run so fast that they can't control the ball. The ball will bounce higher than normal because the kids will be pushing it out in front of them with more force.

Power Dribble (simple) – This is a type of "Controlled Dribble" that is used when a defender is closely guarding the dribbler. Have the kids stand with their backs to the basket and have them perform a controlled dribble with more bend in the knees and the waist and with the off-hand protecting the ball. They should also apply more force during this dribble to make sure the ball is not out of their hand very long. They should pretend that a defender is directly behind them as they dribble. Have the kids dribble backwards toward the basket at a walking pace. After they have backed up several feet, have them switch directions and move away from the basket. Their backs should be facing the basket the entire time. When the kids get the hang of this, have another player stand behind the dribbler and play defense against them to make it more realistic.

Alternating Dribble (moderate) – Have the kids change between "Controlled Dribbles" and bursts of "Speed Dribbles". They must try to maintain control of the ball.

Stop & Go Dribble (moderate) – This drill helps kids maintain control of the ball while suddenly changing speeds. Have the kids dribble at a swift pace and then perform a "Jump Stop" when they get to a certain point on the court – make sure they keep dribbling the entire time. After one or two seconds have them sprint again while dribbling. If the players are lined up side by side, you can have them repeat the stop and go action down the entire court (or half court). Or you can have the players do this drill one at a time in order to make sure they are doing it correctly.

Hesitation Dribble (moderate) – This drill is done just the like the "Stop & Go Dribble", except instead of a "Jump Stop", the player performs a series of stutter steps and momentarily slows (hesitates) their pace before quickly speeding back up. This dribble is intended to throw defenders off balance by fooling them into thinking the dribbler will be completely stopping. If possible, have the players incorporate a slight head and shoulders fake to add to the effectiveness of the hesitation.

Crossover Dribble (moderate) – This is a dribble used to quickly change directions. This dribble is performed by having a player simply dribble with one hand and then quickly bounce the ball in front of their body to the other hand. The player should get down low and should dribble the ball lower than normal to protect it from defenders. Have the kids perform this dribble at a jogging pace and then have them increase their speed as they get comfortable. Put a defender in front of them to make it more realistic.

Pull Back Dribble (moderate) – This dribble is used to back away from the defense and to create space when the defense is applying a high degree of pressure (a double team, for instance). This dribble is performed by having the player quickly advance the ball to a spot on the court and then quickly back away several feet from the spot as if the defense is blocking their path. The ball should remain in the same hand throughout this dribble move and the dribbler should slightly turn their body away from the spot to further protect the ball from defenders.

Pull Back Crossover Dribble (advanced) – This is the same as the basic "Pull Back Dribble", except a "Crossover Dribble" is performed at the moment the player begins to move backward. Since a crossover is utilized, the backward motion should be done at an angle away from the stopping point. For instance, if a player dribbles forward with their right hand, they should crossover to the left hand at the stopping point and then back away to the left at about a 45 degree angle.

Two-Ball Dribble (advanced) – This drill is great for improving dribbling skills with the weak hand. It involves a player dribbling two balls at the same time – one in each hand. They can start out in a stationary position and then move on to walking, jogging, and running. Make sure they are able to maintain control of both balls before speeding up. It will be especially hard for kids to keep their heads up and eyes forward while learning this dribble. You will need to keep reminding them to do so.

Two-Ball Hi-Low Dribble (advanced) – This is an advanced version of the basic "Two-Ball Dribble". During this drill, the players should use as much force as possible with both hands without losing control of the balls. The youth coach should have the players rotate through the following set of dribbles: 1) have them dribble with a very high bounce (the ball should come up to their chests) with both balls hitting the floor at the same time, 2) have them do the same high dribble but with the balls hitting the floor in an alternating pattern, 3) have them dribble with a very low bounce (the ball should stay below the knees) with both balls hitting the floor at the same time, 2) have them do the same low dribble but with the balls hitting the floor in an alternating pattern, 5) have them dribble one ball high and the other ball low at the same time.

Spin Dribble (advanced) – This is an advanced dribble used to evade defenders while maintaining forward progress. This dribble is performed by having a player do a speed dribble to a cone or certain point on the court. If they are dribbling with their right hand, they need to plant their left foot at or near the spot and then quickly pivot their body back and to the right (clockwise) until their right foot has done about a 180 degree rotation and lands on the other side of the spot. The right hand is positioned more on the side of the ball than on the top in order for the ball to be dragged around during the spin. The ball remains in the right hand and is not dribbled until the spin has been completed. Just as the player is completing the spin, they should bounce the ball once with the right hand and then switch to a left-handed dribble. This simulates spinning around a defender while maintaining your dribble. Have the kids start slow and then speed up as they get comfortable. Have a defender stand on the spot to make it more realistic.

Between the Legs Dribble (advanced) – This is an advanced type of "Crossover Dribble" where the ball is bounced between the legs while going from one hand to the other. Since the ball is not bouncing in front of the dribbler, it is better protected from defenders. Have the kids start off slow until they get used to this movement. You can also have them slowly walk down the court while dribbling the ball between their legs on every bounce.

Behind the Back Dribble (advanced) – This is an advanced type of "Crossover Dribble" where the ball is wrapped around the dribblers back with one hand and delivered to the other hand with a quick bounce during the transition. Since the ball is not bouncing in front of the dribbler, it is better protected from defenders. Have the kids start off slow until they get used to this movement.

Passing Drills

Back & Forth Passes (simple) – Have the kids pair up and have them line up on either side of the free throw lane facing each other. Have the kids practice chest passes, bounce passes, side passes, and overhead passes. Make sure to check their passing forms, their accuracy and their catching ability. Give instructions as needed. You can have the kids move closer or farther away depending on their age and ability.

Slide & Pass (simple) – This drill is performed just like the "Back & Forth" pass except the players slide down the court as they make passes to one another. Have the pairs start under the basket and go to mid-court or the full length of the court before returning to the end of the line.

Monkey in the Middle (simple) – This is similar to the "Back & Forth" pass except a defender stands between the two passers and attempts to steal or deflect passes. If a passer has their pass stolen or deflected they become the "monkey" and must act as the defender – the previous "monkey" becomes a passer. The passers cannot throw the ball over the head of the defender. The defender should not just stand in the middle, they need to go back and forth between the passers and apply pressure. The passers should utilize fakes and "Side Passes" to keep the ball away from the defender. The passers must also utilize a pivot foot to avoid traveling. You may need to move the passers closer or farther away to make it harder or easier for the defense.

Speed Passes (moderate) – This drill will help kids become better pass catchers. Have the kids form two lines facing each other at either end of the foul line elbow areas. Using one ball, have the first player in one of the lines make a chest pass to the first person in the other line. As soon as the pass is made, the passer runs to the end of the other line. The receiver then makes a chest pass to the next player in the other line and runs to the end of that line. This continues until the kids have each gone 2 or 3 times. Have them do bounce passes as well. The players should start off slow and then build up the speed of the passes and line changes.

4 Corners (moderate) – This is a great drill for teaching kids about spacing and about the major areas of the court. Place 4 cones in a square configuration: 1 at the right wing, 1 at the left wing, 1 at the left baseline, and 1 at the left baseline. Give a ball to one of the players and have them pass to a player at one of the other positions. As soon as they pass the ball, the player needs to switch places with a player at one of the other positions other than the one they passed to. The player that received the pass, now passes to another player and makes a switch. This continues until the kids get the hang of it and can make quick passes and switches. Explain to the kids that they should be spaced this way during game situations. The switch is meant to simulate setting picks or a simple motion offense.

Fast Break Pass (moderate) – This drill requires the full court. It simulates a player rebounding a ball and making a pass to a teammate sprinting ahead of them to the basket. Split the team into two groups: one lines up under the basket, the other team lines up at mid-court near the right sideline. Throw the ball off of the backboard and have the first player in line under the basket rebound the ball and take off dribbling to the other basket as in a fast break. The first player at mid-court runs toward the other basket and puts their hand up to signal for a pass. The dribbler passes the ball to the player signaling for the ball. Make sure the pass is made before the dribbler crosses the top of the key in the backcourt, and make sure the pass is out in front of the receiving player – they must lead them to the basket with the pass. The receiving player gathers the ball and goes in for a layup.

3-Man Fast Break (moderate) – This is another classic drill that teaches kids proper spacing during fast breaks and transition offenses. This drill can be done in a half court setting, but using the full court is preferable. Have the kids split into three lines: one directly under the basket (the point player), and one on each side of the basket halfway between the free throw lane and the sideline (these are the left and right wing players). The point player dribbles down the court at full speed with the left and right wing players running down the court as well. Make sure all three players stay in their lanes and stay even with each other.

As the players reach the foul line on the other end of the court, the point player stops at the foul line (jump stop) and the wing players angle toward the basket. The point makes a pass (a bounce pass is preferable but a chest pass is acceptable) to one of the wing players, and the wing player takes the ball to the basket for a layup. Make sure all of the kids run the point position at least once. When the kids get comfortable with this drill they can try the "3-Man Weave" described below.

Give & Go Pass (advanced) – This is a classic offensive move. Have the kids form two lines: one at the point area between the top of the key and mid-court, and one at the right wing even with the foul line and a few feet from the sideline. The first player at the point passes the ball to the wing player, makes a quick jab step to the left and cuts immediately to the basket. The wing player catches the ball and quickly passes it back to the player cutting to the basket – a chest pass is probably best as the players may be too close for a bounce pass. The cutter needs to receive the ball near the foul line and continue to the basket for a layup.

Give & Go Handoff (advanced) – This is similar to the "Give & Go" pass except the two lines are formed at the left edge of the point area and at the area between the foul line and the top of the key. The first player at the left point passes the ball to the foul line player, makes a quick jab step to the left and cuts immediately to the right side of the foul line player. The foul line player hands the ball off to the point player and the point player drives to the basket for a layup. In a real game situation, the foul line player actually sets a pick for the point player while handing the ball off, clearing space for an open layup.

3-Man Weave (advanced) – This is a classic passing drill that requires a full court. Have the players form three lines on the baseline: one directly below the basket, one on the left sideline, and one on the right sideline. The sideline players should be about 5 feet inside the sidelines. The first players in each line work together to complete the drill. The player in the middle under the basket has the ball first. As soon as the first pass is made, all three players begin to move down the court together in a simulated fast break. The middle player passes the ball to the right side player and then runs behind that player and takes their place on the right side. While the middle player is running behind the right side player, the right side player is passing the ball to the left side player and then running behind the left side player and taking their place. The left side player then passes the ball to the player that is now on the right and they run behind that player.

This "weaving" of players continues down the court until they are close enough to the opposite basket to complete a layup. They stay at that end of the court until the remaining players have completed the weave. Except for the player going in for the layup, there should be no dribbling. Also, try to have the players remain the same distance apart as they advance down the court. Players tend to move too close together during this drill.

Shooting Drills

Form Shooting (simple) – This is a warm up drill in which kids shoot a ball with proper form straight up into the air a few feet and then catch it. They should be able to catch the ball without moving from the spot where they are standing. They can also do this drill while facing a wall and having the ball bounce off the wall and back to them. This drill enables the kids to focus on their forms without being distracted by the basket. It also helps them become stronger shooters.

Backspins (simple) – This is a variation of the "Form Shooting" drill in which kids shoot a ball up and out in front of them just a few feet while focusing on using proper form. They also need to make sure the ball is rolling off of the finger tips as it is released and the shooting hand snaps down into the follow through position. If this is done correctly, the ball should have some backspin while it is in the air and should actually bounce slightly backwards to the player. Backspin is important for creating a smooth ball flight and for softening the landing if the ball hits the rim. Don't worry too much if the younger kids are not able to do this right away. It is much more important for them to simply get used to getting the ball up to the basket in whatever manner works best for them.

Free Throws (simple) – Have the kids simply line up around the free throw lane (in rebounding position) with one of the players at the free throw line – have them move to the distance that is designated by the league for their age group. Have each player take turns shooting 3-5 free throws while you give them instructions on how to improve their mechanics. If you don't have much time for this drill, you can have the kids shoot only 2 shots before rotating. Have the kids go through 2 or 3 complete rotations and keep track of how many the team makes. Give them a team goal before they start – 30%-60% depending on the age and skill level. If the team doesn't reach their goal they must run laps. If they make their goal, the coach(s) runs the laps.

The form that kids use for free throws will be the foundation for all of their shots (other than layups). Besides the standard mechanics outlined in the "BEEEF" checklist (pg. 36), kids should also try to get a quick feel for the ball and the shot by dribbling a couple of times or spinning the ball in their hands or going through the shooting motion without the ball. It is also important for kids to take their time before shooting by taking one or two deep breaths. This will help them relax. One other thing the kids should do is make sure the lines on the ball are running from side to side – parallel with the floor. This will help ensure proper rotation.

Regardless of what they do to get a feel for the ball or how they get relaxed, the kids should try to do the same routine for all of their free throws. This reinforces the muscle memory of the shots and will greatly improve the kid's accuracy over time. Make sure the kids do not step across the foul line before the ball hits the rim – this is a violation.

No Dribble Layups (simple) – This is a great drill for improving kid's ability to make layups. It allows the kids to focus strictly on the shooting portion of layup instead of the dribbling portion. Have each player get a ball and form a single line a couple of feet from the basket near the low block area. They should be facing the basket at an angle. Have the kids take one step and then go up for a layup. Make sure they attempt to use the backboard by aiming for the square just above and behind the rim – explain to them that the ball has a much greater chance of going in the basket if they use the backboard.

Kids should try to take the ball up for the shot using their shooting hand with the knee on the same side going up during the shot. However, don't worry about the knee position if the kids must have both feet on the floor to get the ball up high enough. A textbook layup should be shot with the hand that is on the same side on which the basket is being approached. If you are approaching the basket from the left side, the left hand should be the shooting hand and vice versa. Don't worry about this until kids become much more skillful at doing layups at full speed with their strong hand.

Dribble Layups (simple) – This is a classic drill. Split the team in half and have single lines form at the left and right wing areas above the free throw line. Give the first player in one of the lines a ball -- most kids are right-handed, so start with the ball on the right side wing. The player with the ball dribbles at an angle (45 degrees) to the basket and shoots a layup off the backboard when they get within a couple of feet of the basket. The first player in the other line (rebounding line) gathers the ball and passes it to the next player in the shooting line. The rebounder goes to the end of the shooting line, and the shooter goes to the end of the rebounding line.

Most kids will have to come to a partial (or even full) stop just prior to shooting. This is fine. It is actually preferable for them to come to a jump stop before shooting the layup if this is the only way for them to maintain control of the ball. A few players will quickly develop the ability to go up for the layup in one continuous motion. This is the goal each player should strive for, but it usually doesn't develop until the 2nd or 3rd grade – be patient. The most important thing is for kids to stay in control and to take a good shot. They can add speed as they get better at making the actual shot.

Dribble Shots (simple) – Have the kids line up just like the "Dribble Layup" drill, but have the kids shoot a jump shot when they get to anywhere from 5-15 feet away from the basket. Since the kids are approaching the basket at an angle, they should attempt to use the backboard on their shots – especially if they get close to the basket. Make sure the kids are taking their time and taking good shots. You can have the kids shoot from different spots around the basket to add some variety.

Pass Layups (moderate) – This is the same as the "Dribble Layup" except the first player in the rebounding line initially has the ball and makes a bounce pass to the first player in the shooting line – the shooter breaks to the basket before the pass is made. Make sure the passes are good – they should lead the shooter toward the basket and arrive in time for the shooter to take a good shot. You may need to move the lines further away from the basket to allow time and space for the pass and the shot.

Pass & Shoot (moderate) – This drill is the same as the "Pass Layups" drill except the kids pull up for a jump shot instead of driving in for a layup. The kids can shoot from 5-15 feet away depending on their age and ability. The kids can be set up to pass and shoot from different locations on the court. Make sure the shooters take their time and get squared up to the basket.

Fast Break Layups (moderate) – Give each player a ball and have them line up under a basket. Have the first player dribble the ball to the basket at the other end of the court and attempt a layup. They should then gather their ball and dribble back to the first basket and shoot another layup before going to the end of the line. The kids should run as fast as they can while maintaining control of the dribble.

Pressure Layups (moderate) – This drill allows kids to get used to shooting layups with the pressure of defenders behind them. Split the team in half and have one line stand under a basket (pressure line) and the other line in the right wing area (layup line) – about halfway between the free throw line and mid-court line. Each player in the pressure line is given a ball. The first player in this line passes the ball to the first player in the layup line. The layup player must immediately take off dribbling toward the opposite basket and attempt a fast break layup. Tell them to focus on the shot and not to worry about anything going on behind them.

The pressure player must attempt to catch up to the layup player and stop the ball or distract them. Shouting, clapping, waving arms and stomping feet are all permitted, but the pressure player must never touch the layup player or cause them to fall. Explain to kids that fouling a player when they are attempting a layup is extremely dangerous and can easily injure the shooter. They should never push, shove, trip, or body block a player during a fast break layup – if they attempt to block a layup they must learn not to plow into the shooter during the attempt. After shooting and pressuring the layup, have the players wait in an area away from the basket until all of the players have come down the court. Have the players switch lines and go through the drill again in the other direction.

Curl Shots (advanced) – This drill develops the coordination necessary to catch a pass, square up to the basket and take a balanced shot. Place a cone on the elbow of the free throw line and have the kids line up on the baseline corner of the foul area diagonal to the cone. The first kid runs up diagonally toward the cone and curls around the cone with their hands up ready to receive a pass. As the player curls around the cone, the coach passes them the ball from the sideline area. The player should complete their curl, get squared up to the basket and take a jump shot. It's okay if the players take a dribble in order to get in the proper position. Make sure the kids don't rush through the steps (catch, square up, balanced shot). You can set up this shot from different areas of the court and at different distances from the basket.

Tunnel Layups (advanced) – This drill combines passing and layups, and requires a full court. Have the players line up on the right side of the baseline, each with a ball. Have coaches/helpers stationed at three different spots on the court: one on the right sideline, halfway between the baseline and mid-court line; one at center court; and one on the right sideline, halfway between mid-court and the far baseline. Have the first player in line pass their ball to the first station and then begin running straight down the court. The first station passes the ball back to the player, who then passes the ball to the second station as they continue down the court. The second station passes the ball back to the player, who passes to the third station. The third station makes a final pass to the player, and they take the ball in for a layup. The players need to dribble the ball as necessary to keep from traveling, but if done properly, dribbling should only be required during the drive to the basket. Have the players perform this drill as fast as possible while making good passes and catches.

Scrimmage Drills

Pass only Scrimmage (simple) – This drill is great for all age groups. It takes the focus off of shooting and forces the offense to work as a team. Form 2 teams and have them play against each other in a scrimmage. You can use a 5-on-5 or 3-on-3 format. The team on offense cannot shoot the ball, and the ball cannot be held by a player for more than 5 seconds. The team on defense must follow the normal league rules (i.e. no stealing the dribble). You can award points for each successful pass by the offense, and for stolen passes and 5-second violations by the defense. If the defense steals the ball or forces a 5-second violation, they gain possession of the ball and play offense. Remind the offensive players to set picks and create good spacing on the court. This drill can be done in a full or half-court setting.

1-on-1 Hustle Drill (simple) – This drill is also great for all age groups. It teaches kids to hustle for loose balls and to hustle on defense. Have the players form two lines, one on either side of the basket at the low block areas on the baseline. Put a ball on the court at the top of the key and yell "go". The kids must sprint to the ball and try to secure it. The player that gains possession of the ball becomes the offensive player, the other must play defense. Both players must hustle for rebounds and the play does not stop until someone scores a basket. Make sure the players in line are evenly matched to prevent one player from dominating another. Also make sure the kids do not get too physical when they scramble for the ball and for rebounds – and they will get physical during this drill.

2-on-2 Scrimmage (simple) – Have four players form two teams and play each other in a live scrimmage. This drill simplifies the game by allowing players to work in a less crowded environment where the basic offensive and defensive actions can be clearly seen and experienced. All aspects of the game should be displayed during this drill: dribbling, shooting, passing, rebounding, on-the-ball and off-the-ball defense, boxing out, setting picks, and communication. Make sure the offensive players are in constant motion, using jab steps and set good picks. Make sure the defenders maintain good defensive position and help each other when necessary. Have the players play non-stop for 3-5 minutes and then bring in a new set of players. This drill is also effective in a 3-on-3 format.

5-on-5 Scrimmage (simple) – This is where you let the players play in a normal game setting. You can have them practice specific offensive plays or defensive assignments. Try to let them play for a while without any instructions and then step in and help them in the areas where they need it. Try not to stop the game flow too much, but do address any areas of concern. You can also give instructions to specific players without stopping play and tell them to make any necessary adjustments on offense and defense as play continues.

3-on-2 Fast Break (advanced) – This drill is just like the "3-Man Fast Break" with the addition of two defenders waiting in the free throw lane of the target basket. The kids will learn how to make decisions based on what the defense does. If the defenders commit to guarding the wing players, the point can either take a short jump shot or take the ball to the basket for a layup. If one of the defenders guards the point player, one of the wings will be open and should receive the pass for a layup or a short shot. The point can also utilize fakes to make the defense move in one direction or another.

12. FUN GAMES TO PLAY

Playing games is a great way to end a practice on a fun note, and to infuse energy during practice by taking breaks from the drills. Many of the games are really drills disguised as games, so the kids have a little more fun while they learn the fundamentals. Playing games is also a good way to have the kids learn how to compete in a low pressure environment. There will be kids that do not respond well to losing – either getting mad and overly aggressive, or possibly crying in frustration. Use those moments to teach kids about good sportsmanship – teach them that it's their effort that matters most, not the outcome of the game. Challenge them to keep trying and shower them with praise when they show improvement.

Dribbling Games

Dribble Tag – Have all of the players spread out over the entire court with a basketball (use half court if necessary) and designate one player as "it". The object of the game is for everyone to maintain their dribble while the "it" player dribbles around and attempts to tag another player. Once a tag is made, the "it" player goes to the sideline and leaves the game. The player that is tagged is now "it" and must tag another player before leaving the game. This is repeated until the last player is tagged. Make sure everyone stays inbounds during the game. If you have a player that is a very good dribbler, you can slow them down by having them dribble with their weak hand only.

Double Dribble Tag – This is similar to "Dribble Tag" above, but there are two players that are designated as "it". Once the "it" players tag another player, the tagged player leaves the game. This is repeated until the last player is tagged.

Dribble Knockout – The object of this game is for players to maintain their dribble within a designated area while they try to knock the ball away from other players that are also dribbling. Players whose basketballs go outside the designated area (for any reason) are out of the game and must sit on the sideline. You can start with all of the players with half of the court as the designated area, and then reduce the boundaries to within the three point area or within the free throw lane area as the number of players is reduced. You can also split the team into two squads and have members of each squad play head to head within the free throw lane. You can impose a 10 or 15 second time limit if the players are not actively trying to knock balls away.

Dribble Relay – Have the players form two lines on either side of the free throw lane. Give the first player in each line a ball. When you say "go", the players dribble to half court or to the other end of the court and then back to the line. They hand the ball to the next player in line and they dribble down next. Have the kids go through the lines twice and see which team finishes first. Make sure the kids maintain control of the ball. You can also set up cones in different configurations and have the teams dribble through them.

Shooting Games

Freeze Out – This game adds more realistic pressure to free throws. Have the kids line up around the free throw lane just like the normal free throw drill. However, they only get one shot. If a player misses their shot, they rotate around with the rest of the players and the next player prepares to shoot. If that player makes their shot, the player that just missed is "frozen out" of the game and must leave the line up and stand out of bounds behind the backboard. Players that make their shots remain in the game and simply rotate around with the rest of the players. "Frozen" players are allowed to distract the shooters (within reason) by making noise and waving their arms – players still in line are not allowed to distract shooters.

Free Throw Talley – This free throw drill requires two different baskets. Form two teams at each basket with one player at the free throw line and the others around the lane in rebounding position. Yell "go", and have the teams begin shooting free throws one player at a time. Made free throws are worth +1 points and misses are worth -2 points. You can also have makes equal +2 and misses equal -1 if the players cannot shoot that well. The drill is over when one team gets to +10 points.

Knock Out – This drill works just like "Freeze Out", except the kids line up behind each other in single file at the free throw line. The first two kids in line are given a ball. The first player in line takes an initial shot from the free throw line, followed quickly by the second player. If the first player misses their initial shot, they must attempt to rebound the ball and make a follow up shot (any shot) before the second player makes a shot. If the first player makes a follow up shot before the second player makes a shot, they must gather the ball, pass it to the next player in line, and run to the end of the line. If the second player makes their initial shot or a follow up shot before the first player makes a shot, the first player is "knocked out" of the game and must pass their ball to the next player in line and sit down on the sidelines. The second player is now in jeopardy of being knocked out of the game by the third player. This continues until there is only one player remaining.

Kids will usually abandon all of the proper shooting techniques to simply get the ball to the basket as quickly as possible. Remind them to take their time and to use proper form. One way to ensure better shooting is to limit each player to only 1 or 2 shots.

Layup/Jump Shot Relay – You need two baskets for this drill. Split the team into two groups and position them in the wing area of two different baskets. Each group has one ball. When you shout "go", the players in each group take turns shooting layups. The game ends when one team gets to 10 made shots. You can also have each team take jump shots from a specific area of the court instead of layups. Remind the kids that this is a game of accuracy and not necessarily speed.

Games Just For Fun

Musical Balls – The players will love this game. Don't let the name full you…this game will really get the kids hustling and diving on the floor after balls. Make sure the kids do not push, trip, or pile on each other. Have the players line up on the baseline, facing away from the basket (no peeking). Spread some balls around the court and make sure there is one less ball than there are players. Yell "go" and have the kids turn around and try to get a ball.

One of the players will not get a ball and must sit down on the sideline. Once the balls have been retrieved have the players put them down, return to the baseline, and turn around again. Take away another ball and spread the rest of them around the court again. Continue this until there is only one player and one ball remaining. To add some humor, the coach can hide the final ball behind their back and under their shirt to confuse the final two players. Once the two players realize where the ball is, it will be hilarious watching them chase down the coach like hungry lions.

First One to… -- This is a good game that you can get creative with. Challenge your players to be the "first one to" accomplish something interesting like: rolling a basketball ball down the court like a bowling ball and trying to hit a cone (this is good for conditioning since the kids must retrieve their ball and run back if they miss the cone); making layups or free throws at every basket and then running to center court; spinning the ball on your finger for 5 seconds; bouncing the ball into the basket. Be creative!

13. OFFENSIVE PLAYS

It is worth repeating….the single most important offensive weapon is the ability to dribble. The better your kids can dribble, the better your offense will be. The ability to create space is also a critical element of team offenses. Players must effectively utilize jab steps to get free of their defenders, and they must properly execute picks to free up their teammates. Once space is created, passing becomes much easier. The ability to shoot is actually the least important offensive ability for young teams. Kids cannot shoot if they cannot get clear of the defense by dribbling, faking, or utilizing solid picks.

Youth coaches should not worry about assigning traditional positions (guards, forwards, centers) to their players. The tallest kids should be expected to dribble the ball like a guard and the smallest players should be expected to go after rebounds like a forward or center. One method of making it easier for kids to learn spacing and to run designed plays is to assign them to one of three different areas on the offensive end of the court: "ones" bring the ball down the court and initiate the offense (point guard); "twos" play in either wing area between the free throw line and sidelines; "threes" play on either side of the basket near the baseline. Players should be interchangeable and should spend equal time playing in all three areas throughout the season.

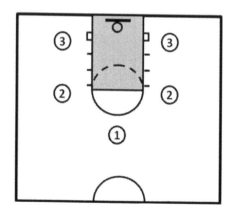

Youth coaches will find it nearly impossible to teach offensive plays to kids in 1st grade and below. Focus on the kid's ability to dribble, hustle after rebounds and loose balls, and maintain good spacing. Encourage kids in this age group to try to set picks for each other – especially for the dribbler. Planned passes will be almost non-existent during games with these kids. Hand-offs and short tosses will be much more common. Take advantage of this by trying to set up a simple offense based on one player running to the ball to receive a football-style hand-off and then dribbling to the basket (Figure 1). The player handing off the ball doesn't necessarily set a pick, but they do get in the way of the defender to help create space.

Figure 1 (Hand-Off)

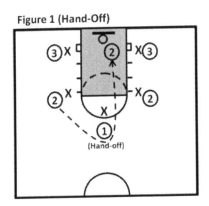

Figure 2 (Basic Pick)

Kids in the 2nd grade will continue to struggle with performing offensive plays, but youth coaches should keep drilling them on the basics. There will typically be a few kids that jump way ahead of others and who can pick up on offensive plays easier. These early bloomers are usually the best scorers. Challenge them to make their teammates better by looking for passing opportunities and setting good picks. Dribbling, passing and setting picks should start to get easier at this age, so one or two additional offensive plays can be added to the initial play in Figure 1. Try introducing a Basic Pick play (Figure 2) and a Give and Go play (Figure 3).

Simply alternating between the Hand-Off play in Figure 1 and the Basic Pick play in Figure 2, can keep most 2nd grade defenses off balance. The Give and Go play has 3 main options: "give and go" to the basket for a potential pass; "give and go" set a pick on the pass receiver; "give and go" get a hand-off from the pass receiver. With just 60 minutes of practice a week, it can be extremely difficult to teach offensive plays along with all of the fundamentals of the game. Do not hesitate to abandon any and all offensive plays if the kids really struggle with them and still need to work on the basics. Learning the fundamentals is much more important than learning specific plays.

Figure 3 (Give & Go)

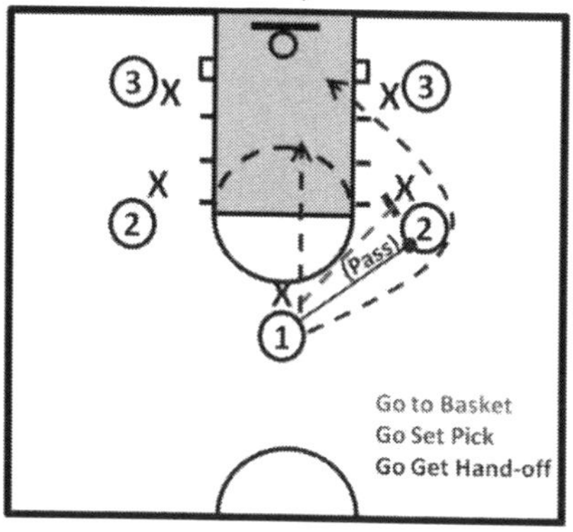

Figure 4 (High Post Give & Go)

Youth coaches with 3rd and 4th grade teams must implement at least 2-4 offensive plays – teach 1-2 plays in 3rd grade and add 1-2 more plays in 4th grade. Many 3rd grade teams will almost exclusively run the Basic Pick play in Figure 2. Running just one play most of the time will allow the defense to adjust and make it difficult to execute the play throughout an entire game. Keep the defense honest by mixing up the Simple Hand-Off with the Basic Pick. Also try to teach the players to set picks from different directions and to fake picks and cut to the basket for passes.

Figure 5 (High Post Give & Go)

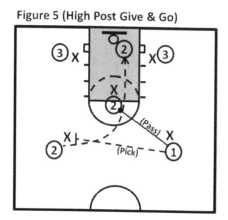

Figure 6 (High Post Back Pick)

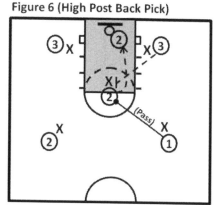

For older teams, there are an endless number of simple plays that can be developed depending on the abilities of your players. One relatively easy and versatile offensive set is to establish a high post player as the focal point of the offense. The high post player either receives the ball from the point guard or sets key picks for others. This set provides numerous options if executed properly. The initial pass to the high post player is the most critical and difficult element of this offense.

If the high post player receives the ball they can execute Give and Go plays (Figure 4 and Figure 5), or have back picks set to allow them to drive to the basket (Figure 6). If they don't receive the ball, the high post player can set a pick for the dribbler (Figure 7) or for another player to set up a pass (Figure 8).

Figure 7 (High Post Ball Pick)   **Figure 8 (High Post Pass Pick)**

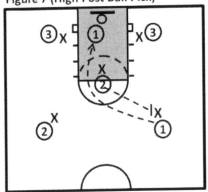
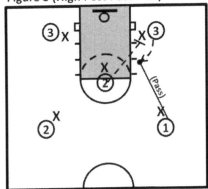

Learning how to play as a team is a long process that starts with learning the fundamentals. Teams will then slowly progress through very simple, one-step plays involving just two players, to plays with three players executing one or two steps, and finally to more complex plays involving all players and multiple steps, such as Down Picks (Figure 9) and Side Picks (Figure 10).

Regardless of the plays you decide to teach, do not expect perfection from the players. In fact, don't expect the plays to be executed nice and neat like the diagrams show. Kids will forget what to do and defenses will make adjustments. Look for understanding by the players of how plays are supposed to work and look for them to understand what their roles are. Results will eventually come so be patient and always praise the player's efforts to learn and push themselves.

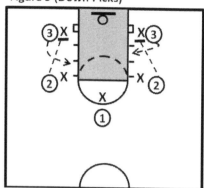

Figure 9 (Down Picks)

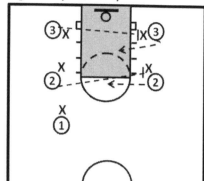

Figure 10 (Side Picks)

Simple Inbound Plays

Inbounding or throwing-in the ball is an important aspect of the offense because it will occur numerous times during games. Don't worry about running inbound plays that are designed to create scoring opportunities. It is much more critical to simply get the ball thrown in without it being stolen and without a 5-second violation being called. Practice the inbound plays to make sure your players know what to expect. Tell the passer not to rush the pass and not to move their feet (inbound violation). Tell the receivers to give the passer a target with their hands and move aggressively to the ball.

Spacing is especially important during inbound plays since the area of play is restricted by the sideline or baseline. Teach kids not to crowd around the player throwing in the ball. Plays should be designed to clear space for one or two players to receive the inbound pass. The other players should work to get open, but should stay clear of the primary play. If the initial play fails, have the players use their bodies to block out their defenders to get open for passes. Don't forget; when the ball is being inbounded on the sideline, you can have a player go to the backcourt to receive a pass.

For 1st grade teams and under, designed plays are not very effective. You can try the "Stack" (Figure 11) formation and then tell them to move quickly in all directions to try to get open for a pass. This formation is also the primary play used for inbounding the ball on the sideline. Older youth teams should only have 1 or 2 inbound plays and they should be very simple. The plays detailed below are classic inbound sets that should be easy to teach. The first is the "Stack" which involves the kids lining up in single file and then moving to open areas of the court. The other classic set is the "Box". This play involves the players forming a box around the free throw lane and then setting side picks (Figure 12) or up picks (Figure 13) to get players open.

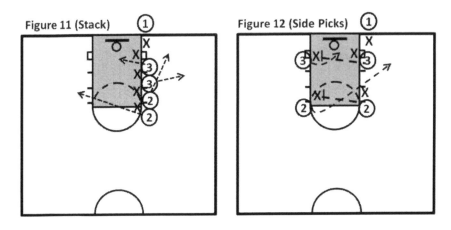

Figure 11 (Stack)   Figure 12 (Side Picks)

Another effective inbound play that can also create a quick scoring opportunity is the "Box Out" (Figure 14). This play is set up just like the "Box". The low post players jab step toward the free throw line as if they are going to set an up pick and then they pivot around their defenders and box them out. They should have their hands up and ready to receive a pass. They should be in position for a layup or a short shot right in front of the basket. The high post players should switch sides and flare down and out to receive a pass if the primary play does not work.

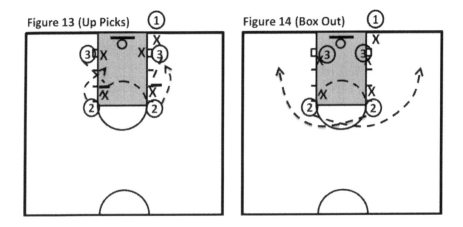

Figure 13 (Up Picks)   Figure 14 (Box Out)

PART 3: DEFFENSE & REBOUNDING

Most youth leagues do not allow zone defenses. Therefore, this guidebook only addresses "Man-to-Man" (or "man") defense. Furthermore, players must play good man defense in order to become good overall defenders. When teaching young players about defense you must keep it simple: players must stay between the player they are guarding and the basket and must always know where the ball is. The defensive concepts outlined below explain the textbook method of playing defense. The vast majority of kids under 10 years old will not be able to play this level of defense on a consistent basis. It takes too much stamina and concentration for most of them. Focus on teaching young kids to stay between their man and the basket, to always know where the ball is, and most importantly, to hustle at all times. This will lay the proper foundation for later advancements.

Most kids tend to use their hands and arms to play defense, but good defense is played with the feet. Players must maintain a wide stance (shoulder width) on the balls of their feet with their knees bent close to 45 degrees – this stance is very tiring and most young players cannot maintain it very long. They must try to stay balanced and not lean their head too far in any direction – the head should be up with the eyes forward. The back should remain straight and the hands should be up and ready to deflect passes or block shots. Many youth leagues don't allow stealing the ball while it is being dribbled until the 3rd grade. This makes foot work even more important.

Most kids also tend to blindly follow their man around the court, oblivious to where the ball is and oblivious to oncoming picks. Teach kids to always know where the ball is and teach them that it is fine to leave their man if they need to stop another player that has gotten open with the ball. Also teach kids to be on the lookout for picks and to try to avoid them either by fighting through them or by going around the pick. Fighting through picks simply means squeezing between the offensive players and not allowing the picker to block them. Going around a pick means dropping back and moving around the picker to the spot their player is likely to end up. If players decide to go around the pick they must be careful not to move too soon and give their man a clear lane to the basket and possibly an easy layup.

Eventually kids should be taught to switch on picks. This involves having the two defensive players involved in a pick switching the offensive players they are guarding. Switching requires good communication between teammates as the defender whose man is setting the pick needs to first call out the pick and then needs to yell "switch" to let the player being picked know to guard the other offensive player (the one setting the pick).

Most kids that are 7 years old and under will not be coordinated enough to play even a basic level of defense. It is most important for them to hustle and try to stay close to their man. They must also get used to some amount of physical contact. Many will avoid contact and continuously back away from their man. Encourage them to stand their ground and challenge them to keep their man away from the basket. One of the biggest challenges for kids in this age group is simply remembering who they are supposed to be guarding. The "Wristband Method" described below is the perfect solution.

The Wristband Method

1. Obtain 5 sets of wristbands with 5 different colors.
2. The 5 players on offense are given one wristband to wear, each with a different color.
3. The 5 players on defense are given the other wristbands to wear, with the color matching the color of the man they will be guarding – the offensive player wearing the black wristband is guarded by the defensive player wearing the matching black wristband, and vice versa.
4. Just prior to games, find the opposing coach, explain this method of helping the kids to know who to guard, and ask if they would agree to use the wristbands – most will not only agree, but will love the idea.
5. As players go out of the game, have them hand over their wristband to the player going into the game.
6. Rearrange the wristbands as needed to make sure you match up the kids appropriately.
7. Don't forget to get the wristbands back after the game.

☆ The wristbands can be used as year-end awards for the kids as they achieve their Star Chart goals.

---

14. HOW TO DEFEND

On-the-Ball Defense

When guarding a player with the ball, the defender must get into the defensive stance – a wide stance with the feet slightly flared outward; knees bent to about a 45-degree angle; back straight enough to keep the head from going forward past the knees and; hands up and ready to block any passes or shots. The defender should maintain a gap between the offensive player until they get within shooting distance of the basket. The gap is necessary to allow the defender time to react to a sudden move by the offensive player. If the defender is too close, it is easier for the offensive player to get around them. The amount of gap depends on how far the player is from the basket – the closer the offensive player gets to the basket the closer they should be defended. Defenders guarding the ball should watch the offensive players mid-section to determine which way they are moving. Offensive players can fake with their head, hands, and feet, but they can't go anywhere without the middle of their bodies.

Most youth leagues do not allow defense to be played until the offense crosses the mid-court line and most kids start guarding their men as soon as they cross half court. Unless your team is "pressing" the offense to try and create a turnover (rare at this age), have the kids back away from mid-court and guard their men when they get closer to the top of the key or foul line area. Many youth leagues have a maximum gap (usually 5 or 6 feet) that defenders cannot exceed while guarding their men – this helps ensure a man-to-man defense is being played. Double teaming offensive players is usually prohibited as well unless the ball enters the free throw lane. You must honor your leagues guidelines and have your players defend accordingly.

Defenders should always try to force dribblers to go in the direction of their weak hand by establishing a position on the strong side of the offensive player. The defender should be at an angle to the offensive player where the foot closest to the offensive player is outside that player's strong side foot. The angle should close as the offensive player gets closer to the basket – they should be directly in front of the player once they are within shooting range. Forcing players to their weak side is especially effective on young players as most cannot dribble the ball that well with their weak hand. Defenders should also try to force players toward the sidelines and baselines to keep the ball out of the middle of the floor where there is more space.

As offensive players dribble the ball, the defender should keep their hands up, their back straight, their knees bent and slide their feet using quick, short steps. They should not cross their feet. If a defender needs to move backwards at an angle to cut off a dribbler, they should perform a drop step. This is done by taking a step back toward the baseline (dropping the foot back) at about a 45 degree angle. They should repeat the drop step until they catch up with the dribbler and are squarely in front of them.

If the dribbler gets past the defender and has an open lane to the basket, the defender needs to get out of the defensive stance and sprint back to catch up with the dribbler. When a defender gets beat by the dribbler, they should first yell "help" to alert his teammates and have them help stop the dribbler. If they are able to get back in front of the dribbler they need to resume the defensive stance.

Defenders guarding the player with the ball should try to avoid reaching for the ball or slapping down in an attempt to steal or deflect the ball. Reaching will cause them to lose their balance and slapping down will often lead to a defensive foul. If a defender wants to go for the ball they should swipe upwards with their hands. Young players will be quite often tempted to steal the ball. Remind them to use their feet to play defense and only go for the ball when it is directly in front of them or they have a clear path to it.

If a player stops dribbling, the defender should immediately establish a position in front of the offensive player, blocking their view of the basket by standing taller with their hands up. The defender must get as close as possible without pushing too much on the offensive player – it's fine to make some contact, but make sure the kids don't lean in too much. The hands should remain active and stay in front of the ball to prevent passes and shots.

Off-the-Ball Defense

Defenders that are guarding offensive players without the ball are said to be playing defense "off-the-ball". They need to position themselves to be able to deny passes to the player they are guarding and to be able to leave their man and help defend players with the ball that get open for shots or drives to the basket. They must do this while staying between their man and the basket and knowing where the ball is at all times. This takes a great deal of time and practice to learn. Players that stand too close to their man can deny the pass, but cannot help their teammates. Players that stand too far away from their man can help on defense, but cannot deny the pass.

How close defenders guard offensive players without the ball depends on how close the ball is to the offensive player as well as how close the player is to the basket. Offensive players are said to be 1 pass away from the ball when they have a direct line of site to the ball with no other players in between. Defenders must guard this type of player by placing their foot slightly forward with their back turned slightly to the ball. The hand nearest the ball should be up with the palm facing the ball – the arm should be held straight at shoulder height. The hand is up to deny any potential passes. As the offensive players move around the court, the defender must maintain this position as long as their man is within 1 pass of the ball. The defender must also stay in position to see both their player and the ball – some degree of peripheral vision is required to do this.

An offensive player is said to be 2 passes way from the ball when they do not have a direct line of site to the ball because there are other offensive players in between. Defenders must guard these players by dropping back until they are able to see their man and the ball – forming a triangle. They should have their ball-side hand up and ready to deflect/stop any passes. This allows the defender to be in position to fall back to help protect the basket and to deny a long pass to their man. The defender must keep moving their feet in order to maintain the triangle.

Defenders playing off the ball need to be able to make quick adjustments on the move. They must be prepared to guard their man as they move between being 2 passes away, 1 pass away, and having the ball. They also need to be able to leave their man and help on defense, and then get back to their man again. Playing good defense is all about quickly reacting to the movement of the ball and the players. It takes a tremendous amount of hustle and concentration.

Transition Defense

At the moment a team on offense loses possession of the ball to the other team, they transition immediately to defense. Since most leagues do not allow teams to play defense in the backcourt, it is very important for players to transition quickly back to defend the basket. Teach kids that the most important thing they need to do as a team is stop the ball from advancing to the basket – regardless of whose man has the ball. Transitioning back on defensive is not typically an issue on made baskets and violations that require the ball to be inbounded by the other team. Teams have plenty of time to get back under these circumstances. However, transition defense must occur very quickly after steals and rebounds by the other team – there is normally a mad dash by all players down the court with no real organization. Most young kids make the critical mistake of only looking for the man they are guarding without regard for where the ball is. This often leads to easy layups by the other team.

Teach the kids to stop the ball first and then find their man. When the team needs to get back on defense in a hurry, the players (and coach) need to yell "back" and sprint to the free throw lane around their basket regardless of where their man is. This will help ensure the area in front of the basket is blocked and the ball is stopped (you may need to adjust this strategy if your league rules do not allow this type of transition defense). If the ball has been stopped by a teammate, they should find their man and guard them appropriately. If the ball has not been stopped, they need to attempt to stop it themselves. Tell kids that defense is a team effort and it is everyone's job to know where the ball is and to stop the ball if an offensive player gets open. The communication tips below will help reinforce the team defense concept.

Communication

Communication is very important while playing defense. The four most critical times defenders need to communicate are:

1. When the offensive player dribbling the ball beats their defender and is open to take a shot or drive to the basket. The defender that is beaten should yell "help" to alert his teammates and have at least one of them leave their man and stop the dribbler. This is one of the reasons defensive players should always know where the ball is – they should be ready to help before being alerted.

2. When a defender's man is preparing to set a pick on another defensive player. The player guarding the picker should yell "pick" to alert his teammate that a pick is coming. The player being picked can take steps to avoid the pick or ready themselves for the contact. One of the defenders can also yell "switch" which means the players should switch the players they are guarding – the player being picked stays with the picker, and the other player stays with the offensive player the pick is being set for. The decision to switch is often predetermined by the coach in their overall defensive strategy.

3. When a player takes a shot, all of the defenders that see the shot should yell "shot". This will alert the defenders to box out their opponents and get into position to rebound the ball.

4. When the defense gets a rebound, the offense suddenly becomes the defense. At this point the new defenders should yell "back" to alert each other to get back on defense and to stop the ball from advancing to the basket.

15. REBOUNDING

Rebounding is the simple act of securing possession of the ball after a missed shot – it's easier said than done. Rebounding is all about hustle and effort. It is also about boxing out, body position, and timing. Most kids are able to get to the ball, but often fail to secure the ball because their hands are not strong enough or they are too timid – they are not used to physical contact. This is perfectly normal. Use some of the rebounding drills in this guidebook to get kids more involved. The "1-on-1 Hustle" and "Musical Balls" drills are also good for getting kids used to contact and used to going after the ball aggressively.

Getting into rebounding position is referred to as "Boxing Out" and is similar to the "posting up" position described earlier – players maneuver in front of an opposing player with their backside pushing the player away from the basket. Players should have their feet wide, their knees slightly bent, their arms up and bent at the elbows, their heads up with their eyes on the ball and their hands up and open ready to grab the ball. Players should jump to the ball and not wait for it to come to them.

How to Rebound:
- Always know where the ball is – on offense and defense. If players don't see that the ball has been shot, they cannot get the rebound.
- Get your body into position to rebound by "Boxing Out" the player closest to you. Boxing out is normally associated with defensive players, but offensive players should attempt to box out as well.
- If the ball comes close to you, go up strong and make yourself as tall as possible, and come down with both feet wide and knees bent.
- Secure the ball firmly with both hands in front of your chest with your elbows flared out to the sides to keep defenders away. Never bring the ball down low as it will be more vulnerable to steals.
- If the offensive player gets the rebound they should attempt to quickly go straight up with a shot before the defense gets set.
- If the rebound is defensive, the player should not just blindly start to dribble. They should look for a clear path to dribble and they should always keep their head up, looking for open teammates and defenders.
- Everyone should assume all shots will be missed and get in position to rebound. This is especially true for the player that shoots the ball. They should always follow their shot and get in position to rebound.

16. DEFENSE & REBOUNDING DRILLS

"Back" Drill (simple) – You can surprise the players with this drill at anytime during practice. First, explain to kids the importance of always running back as fast as possible during transition defense. During practice, you can yell "back" at any time and have the kids run to the free throw lane area nearest to you. If the players do not seem to be giving a full effort to get to the lane, have them run a lap(s) or yell "back" again and have them sprint to the free throw lane at the other end of the court.

Happy Feet (simple) – This drill teaches kids the basic defensive stance and is meant as a conditioning activity. This drill is very fatiguing and should not be done too long. Make sure kids get a water break after it is over. Start by having the players stand side to side with at least an arms-length distance between them – you may need to split them into two lines, one behind the other. Then have the players get into the proper defensive stance with their feet spread wide and their knees bent in a squat position. Make sure they keep their backs straight, heads up, and hands up with elbows bent. Next, have the kids stand on the balls of their feet and begin tapping their feet on the floor rapidly, one foot after the other. The kids will quickly get tired and begin to stand straight up or bend over at the waist. Don't let them get out of the proper defensive position. After about 10 seconds tell them to stop and rest for about 5 seconds. After 5 seconds, tell them to "tap" again for 10 seconds. Repeat this until they have done about 5 sets of taps.

Defensive Slides (simple) – This drill teaches kids how to slide in different directions while in the proper defensive stance. Start by having the players get into the same lineup and stance as described in the "Happy Feet" drill. Instead of tapping their feet, have the players slide to the left or right by pointing in that direction. Have them do about 5 slides to the left and the 5 slides back to the right. Continue to go back and forth for 30-60 seconds. Make sure they do not cross their feet and make sure they maintain the proper defensive stance for the entire time.

Zig-Zag Slides (moderate) – This drill teaches kids how to slide at an angle (drop step) in the defensive stance. First, have the kids pair up and have each pair spread out along the baseline. Give one of the players from each pair a ball. The player with the ball then begins to dribble at an angle to the right or left for a few feet and then crosses over and dribbles in the other direction for a few feet – in a zig-zag pattern. The player without the ball stands in front of the other player, gets in the proper defensive stance, and slides down the court while keeping the dribbler in front of them. The dribbler is not trying to beat the defender – they are simply providing the defender with a target to track down the court. The defender should not steal or deflect the ball – they are practicing their defensive positioning. The players should continue in this manner until they get to the mid-court line or the other baseline. Have them switch places at that point.

Defensive Movement (advanced) – This drill is designed to take players through all of the defensive movements that occur when changing from "on-the-ball" to "off-the-ball", and to help defense. Have the players get into a 5-on-5 format with the offense in a standard formation: point guard, two wings, and two baseline players. Have the ball passed around to each offensive player and have the defense move into the appropriate defensive position depending on where the ball is. The defense is not trying to steal the ball; they simply need to change their positions as the ball moves from player to player. Remind the defenders of the proper stance and position when their man has the ball, when their man is one pass away, and when their man is two passes away. Also, have some of the offensive players drive past their defenders to see if other players help on defense.

Rebound & Shoot (simple) – Have the kids line up at the free throw line in single file. The first player steps forward a few feet and the coach throws the ball off the backboard. The player must take a strong jump toward the ball, catch the ball firmly with both hands and immediately take a shot (make sure they use the backboard). If they drop the ball you can have them run a lap or do 5 pushups on the side before getting back in line (optional).

Team Rebounds (simple) – This drill will really bring out the hustle in the players and teach them what level of physical contact can be expected. Make sure the players do not push, trip, wrestle, hit, or do anything in an aggressive manner directed at another player. Once a player has secured the ball, don't allow the other kids to fight over it or pile on each other.

Have the players line up around the free throw lane in rebounding positions. The coach shoots a free throw and all of the kids go for the rebound. You can add a twist to this drill by rewarding the rebounder with the free throw attempt – whoever gets the rebound gets to take the next free throw. You can also split the players into two teams and have the team that does not get the rebound run a lap(s). Encourage the kids to box out, but this drill is more about effort and hustle, not necessarily mechanics.

2-on-2 Rebounds (advanced) – This drill helps kids focus on boxing out. Have the players pair up. Have one of the pairs line up on one side of the free throw lane and another pair on the other side. The players closest to the basket are considered defenders and other two players are considered offense. The coach should take a free throw shot and have the defenders box out the other players. All of the players should go after the rebound. After a few rebounds, have the players switch places. Continue to do this until all of the players have been able to perform box outs.

PART 4: THE "STAR CHART"

The "Star Chart" system is the perfect tool for establishing and tracking goals related to effort and behavior. It is simple and designed specifically to motivate and reward kids based on their individual ability levels. It consists of a basic chart with specific basketball skills listed across the top and the names of each player down the left side. Below is a sample chart:

STAR CHART								
	Dribbling	Rebounding	Passing	Shooting	Sportsmanship	Hustle	Teamwork	Defense
Andrew								
Jake								
Joe								
Landon								
Lucas								
Luke								
Sam								
Will								
Wyatt								
Team								

The expectation is not for each player to perform at the same level. Each player has different strengths and weaknesses and they should be evaluated based on their individual progress. Therefore, "stars" are awarded as each player displays a certain level of personal improvement in each area. When all of the players receive stars for one of the categories, the "Team" is given a star for that category as well. Below is a sample chart with some awarded stars.

71

STAR CHART

	Dribbling	Rebounding	Passing	Shooting	Sportsmanship	Hustle	Teamwork	Defense
Andrew	★							
Jake				★				
Joe			★					
Landon	★							
Lucas				★				
Luke						★		
Sam				★				
Will		★						
Wyatt					★			
Team								

Here are some tips on how to make the most of the "Star Chart":

☆ The chart should NEVER be used in a negative manner and stars should NEVER be taken away once they have been awarded.

☆ Begin awarding stars after the first game and award them throughout the season until EVERYONE has a star for each category. This is not an MVP award – it is designed to promote team work and celebrate the accomplishments of each player.

☆ Try to award only 1 star at a time for each player. Exceptions can be made if a player misses a game or if the game schedule dictates awarding more than one star.

☆ You do not need to time it so that the kids earn all of their stars at the same time. You should time it so that small groups of players earn their final stars at different times during the final part of the season.

☆ Stars should be awarded based on achievements during games AND practices.

☆ Stars should be awarded only when earned. However, you may need to be creative for kids that struggle in certain areas.

☆ If possible, award the stars right after each game in front of the team and the parents. Make this ceremony very positive and celebratory.

This will draw everyone's attention away from who won or lost the game and focus their attention on the effort given during the game.

★ Award stars early for the strengths of each player. If a player is a great shooter, their first star should be for shooting. This will motivate them to focus on other areas of the game.

★ Try to award stars for the more intangible skills (hustle, teamwork and sportsmanship) in the latter part of the season. This will motivate the players to work on these character building skills throughout the season.

★ Call special attention to the improved efforts of kids that are struggling with a particular skill. This will give them a much needed boost in self-confidence.

★ You have the option of awarding kids a prize when they earn all of their stars. A wrist band, or a customized certificate, or even just a candy bar can add extra excitement and motivation. You also have the option of letting the players know that they will earn a year-end pizza party when the "Team" earns all of their stars. Most teams have parties anyway, but this turns it into a performance incentive.

PART 5: PRACTICE PLANS

Practices should be conducted using one of the 60-minute Practice Plans on the following pages. There are hundreds of drills available to coaches, and the variety can be overwhelming. The drills in the Practice Plans are the same drills described in this guidebook and they are proven to yield the desired results within the short time frame most youth teams have. There are 15 total plans with 3 plans for each of the 5 different grade levels from Pre-School through 4th Grade.

The plans are designed to take kids through a natural progression of fundamental skill development that is specific to their grade level. You can modify the sequence or length of certain drills as needed, and you can mix and match drills to suit your team's needs. Furthermore, your 2nd grade team might need to back up a little and do one of the 1st grade plans, or move forward by doing a 3rd grade plan. It is not an exact science, so coaches need to evaluate their progress and choose plans and drills accordingly. While the plans stop at 4th grade, most of the drills are suitable for all grades beyond 4th; they teach fundamental skills necessary at all levels of play.

While most of the drills can be performed in a half-court setting, better results will usually be achieved with the use of a full-court. If nothing else, it gives the players an opportunity to get up and down the court and improve their cardiovascular endurance. Unfortunately, most youth coaches have limited access to gyms and often must share gym space with other teams. Contact your league administrators to find out which practice days and times offer the best chance of getting a full court. This will likely require some flexibility on the part of the coach and the families. While having a full-court is not too critical for the youngest players, it is a huge advantage for the older kids.

17. THE FIRST PRACTICE

The first practice is critical. It will allow you to communicate your goals and expectations and to set the proper tone for all future practices. The following is a checklist of how the first practice should be conducted.

1. Be prepared for practice – always have a plan.
2. Get to practice early -- always.
3. Personally greet each parent and each player as they arrive.
4. Once everyone has arrived, have the parents come together for a brief meeting. Let the kids shoot around on their own or give them different activities or games to do during the meeting. (The parent meeting is discussed in "Working With Parents" pg. 17.)
5. After the meeting with the parents, huddle the kids together and introduce yourself and your assistant coach(s). Let them know they will have a great deal of fun and learn a lot as long as they follow these four simple rules: 1. Listen to the coaches; 2. Play hard (hustle); 3. Display good sportsmanship; and 4. Have fun.
6. Have the kids introduce themselves to the group. (To help remember names you may want to write the kid's names on name tags and apply them to the front of their shirts for the first practice.)
7. Ask the kids for team name suggestions and take a quick vote. You make the final decision and put that behind you quickly. Or -- just pick a name yourself and go with it.
8. Have the team put their hands in the middle of the huddle, count to three, and have everyone shout the team name. Do it again until it is load and enthusiastic.
9. During the first practice you will want to get an assessment of the skill level of each player by having them go through the basic drills below (refer to the page numbers for descriptions of each drill). You can provide some simple instructions, but don't worry too much about teaching the proper techniques at this time. Just spend a couple of minutes on each drill and make sure to give the kids a couple of water breaks. The drills are as follows:

Drill #	K-1st Grade	2nd-4th Grade
1	Ball Toss & Ball Spins (pg.38)	Wrap Arounds (pg.39)
2	Back & Forth Passes (pg.44)	Back & Forth Passes (pg.44)
3	Spot Dribble (pg.40)	Dribble Relay (pg.53)
4	Dribble Relay (pg.53)	Defensive Slides (pg.68)
5	Happy Feet (pg.68)	No Dribble Layups (pg.47)
6	No Dribble Layups (pg.47)	Rebound & Shoot (pg.69)
7	Rebound & Shoot (pg.69)	Knockout (pg.53)
8	Musical Balls (pg.54)	Musical Balls (pg.54)

[TIP -- It is helpful to "grade" the players in six basic categories – dribbling, shooting, passing, rebounding, hustle, and defense. Give each player a 1-5 score for each category with 5 being the best score. It is important to keep these scores to yourself as you do not want to hurt any player feelings or ruffle the feathers of any parents (including assistant coaches). Use the scores to determine strengths and weaknesses and adjust them throughout the season to track progress. Also refer to the scores when pairing kids up or putting teams together to keep things well balanced.]

10. If time permits, take a few minutes towards the end of practice to go through the basic concepts, rules and terminology of basketball (see "Basketball 101" pg. 82). Also cover the special rules unique to your league (no stealing the dribble, for instance). Continuously reinforce the rules/terms throughout each practice and game during the season.

11. End every practice with a final huddle where you praise the kids with enthusiastic comments about their effort during practice. Also ask them to continue to work on the basics (especially dribbling) at home. Break the huddle with a final "1, 2, 3 GO (*team name*)!!"

12. Always be the last one to leave the gym and ensure that each child is picked up by their parents.

18. PRE-SCHOOL PRACTICE PLANS

Plan #1		
Pg.	ACTIVITY	TIME
40	Dribble Laps	5 min.
	Break	1 min.
82	Basic Rules & Terms	5 min.
38	Ball Toss	5 min.
39	Ball Spins	
	Break	1 min.
40	Spot Dribble	5 min.
41	Controlled Dribble	
54	Musical Balls	5 min.
	Break	1 min.
68	Back Drill	
68	Happy Feet	5 min.
68	Defensive Slides	
44	Back & Forth Passing	5 min.
	Break	1 min.
46	Form Shooting	
46	Backspins	15 min.
47	Free Throws	
47	No Dribble Layups	
	Break	1 min.
53	Knock Out	5 min.

Plan #2		
Pg.	ACTIVITY	TIME
40	Cone Dribble	5 min.
	Break	1 min.
40	Spot Dribble	
40	V-Dribble	5 min.
41	Controlled Dribble	
53	Dribble Relay	5 min.
	Break	1 min.
46	Form Shooting	5 min.
47	No Dribble Layups	
44	4 Corners	5 min.
	Break	1 min.
69	Rebound & Shoot	5 min.
69	Team Rebounds	5 min.
	Break	1 min.
50	1-on-1 Hustle Drill	5 min.
50	Pass Only Scrimmage	10 min.
59	Inbounds Plays	
	Break	1 min.
53	Knock Out	5 min.

Plan #3		
Pg.	ACTIVITY	TIME
40	Cone Dribble	5 min.
	Break	1 min.
39	Wrap Arounds	2 min.
41	Speed Dribble	3 min.
	Break	1 min.
44	Back & Forth Passing	8 min.
44	Slide & Pass	
54	First one to....	2 min.
	Break	1 min.
48	Dribble Layups	5 min.
54	Layup Relay	5 min.
	Break	1 min.
59	Inbounds Plays	
55	Offensive Plays	20 min.
51	5-on-5 Scrimmage	
	Break	1 min.
54	Musical Balls	5 min.

19. 1ST GRADE PRACTICE PLANS

Plan #1		
Pg.	ACTIVITY	TIME
39	Ball Spins	5 min.
39	Wrap Arounds	
40	Spot Dribble	
40	V-Dribble	5 min.
41	Controlled Dribble	
54	Musical Balls	5 min.
	Break	1 min.
68	Defensive Slides	5 min.
68	Zig-Zag Slides	
	Break	1 min.
44	Monkey in the Middle	5 min.
69	Team Rebounds	5 min.
	Break	1 min.
46	Form Shooting	
47	Free Throws	10 min.
47	No Dribble Layups	
50	1-on-1 Hustle Drill	5 min.
	Break	1 min.
53	Knock Out	5 min.

Plan #2		
Pg.	ACTIVITY	TIME
41	Controlled Dribble	5 min.
41	Speed Dribble	
	Break	1 min.
38	Basic Pick	10 min.
	Break	1 min.
69	Defensive Movement	10 min.
	Break	1 min.
55	Offensive Plays	
59	Inbound Plays	15 min.
51	5-on-5 Scrimmage	
	Break	1 min.
54	Layup/Shooting	5 min.

Plan #3		
Pg.	ACTIVITY	TIME
41	Stop & Go Dribble	5 min.
69	Team Rebounds	5 min.
	Break	1 min.
38	Basic Pick	5 min.
69	Defensive Movement	5 min.
	Break	1 min.
51	2-on-2 Scrimmage	10 min.
	Break	1 min.
55	Offensive Plays	
59	Inbounds Plays	15 min.
51	5-on-5 Scrimmage	
	Break	1 min.

20. 2ND GRADE PRACTICE PLANS

Plan #1		
Pg.	ACTIVITY	TIME
40	Cone Dribble	5 min.
	Break	1 min.
39	Wrap Arounds	3 min.
40	Spot Dribble	5 min.
40	V-Dribble	
53	Dribble Relay	3 min.
	Break	1 min.
68	Defensive Slides	
68	Zig-Zag Slides	5 min.
44	Slide & Pass	
44	Speed Pass	5 min.
69	Team Rebounds	5 min.
	Break	1 min.
46	Back Spins	
47	Free Throws	
47	No Dribble Layups	15 min.
49	Fast Break Layups	
	Break	1 min.
50	1-on-1 Hustle Drill	5 min.
53	Knock Out	5 min.

Plan #2		
Pg.	ACTIVITY	TIME
42	Hesitation Dribble	5 min.
	Break	1 min.
69	Rebound & Shoot	5 min.
41	Speed Dribble	5 min.
41	Stop & Go Dribble	
52	Dribble Knock Out	3 min.
	Break	1 min.
37	Jab/Cut Basic	
37	Basic Jump Stop	10 min.
38	Basic Pick	
48	Dribble Shots	5 min.
49	Pressure Layups	
	Break	1 min.
69	Defensive Movement	10 min.
	Break	1 min.
54	First one to...	3 min.
59	Inbound Plays	10 min.
55	Offensive Plays	

Plan #3		
Pg.	ACTIVITY	TIME
41	Stop & Go Dribble	5 min.
69	2-on-2 Rebounds	5 min.
	Break	1 min.
38	Basic Pick	
37	Triple Threat Yells	10 min.
37	Jab/Cut Layup	
	Break	1 min.
59	Inbound Plays	
55	Offensive Plays	32 min.
51	5-on-5 Scrimmage	
	(with breaks)	
	Break	1 min.
54	Musical Balls	5 min.

79

21. 3RD GRADE PRACTICE PLANS

Plan #1		
Pg.	**ACTIVITY**	**TIME**
40	Cone Dribble	5 min.
	Break	1 min.
40	V-Dribble	7 min.
41	Power Dribble	
52	Dribble Tag	3 min.
	Break	1 min.
68	Zig-Zag Slides	3 min.
69	Team Rebounds	7 min.
	Break	1 min.
46	Form Shooting	5 min.
47	Free Throws	
50	1-on-1 Hustle Drill	5 min.
	Break	1 min.
37	Jab/Cut Basic	
37	Jab/Cut Layup	10 min.
37	Triple Threat Yells	
44	Speed Pass	5 min.
	Break	1 min.
54	Musical Balls	5 min.

Plan #2		
Pg.	**ACTIVITY**	**TIME**
42	Crossover Dribble	5 min.
49	Pressure Layups	5 min.
	Break	1 min.
38	Basic Pick & Roll	5 min.
69	Defensive Movements	10 min.
	Break	1 min.
55	Offensive Plays	15 min.
	Break	1 min.
59	Inbounds Plays	17 min.
51	2-on-2 Scrimmage	

Plan #3		
Pg.	**ACTIVITY**	**TIME**
42	Pull Back Dribble	5 min.
49	Curl Shots	5 min.
	Break	1 min.
59	Inbound Plays	
55	Offensive Plays	43 min.
51	5-on-5 Scrimmage	
	(with breaks)	
	Break	1 min.
53	Freeze Out	5 min.

22. 4TH GRADE PRACTICE PLANS

Plan #1		
Pg.	ACTIVITY	TIME
42	Crossover Dribble	5 min.
42	Pull Back Crossover	5 min.
	Break	1 min.
37	Dribble/J-Stop/Pivot/Pass	10 min.
37	Jab/Cut Layup	
68	Defensive Slides	5 min.
68	Zig-Zag Slides	
	Break	1 min.
44	Speed Pass	10 min.
46	3-Man Weave	
54	Shooting Relay	5 min.
	Break	1 min.
59	Inbound Plays	
55	Offensive Plays	17 min.
50	1-on-1 Hustle Drill	

Plan #2		
Pg.	ACTIVITY	TIME
43	Spin Dribble	5 min.
42	Two Ball Dribble	5 min.
50	Tunnel Layups	5 min.
	Break	1 min.
38	Basic Pick & Roll	5 min.
69	2-on-2 Rebounds	5 min.
	Break	1 min.
69	Defensive Movements	10 min.
	Break	1 min.
45	3-Man Fast Break	5 min.
59	Inbound Plays	
55	Offensive Plays	17 min.
51	5-on-5 Scrimmage	
	(with break)	

Plan #3		
Pg.	ACTIVITY	TIME
51	3-on-2 Fast Break	10 min.
	Break	1 min.
49	Curl Shots	10 min.
50	Tunnel Layups	
	Break	1 min.
59	Inbound Plays	
55	Offensive Plays	38 min.
51	5-on-5 Scrimmage	
	(with breaks)	

PART 6: BASKETBALL 101

Youth basketball coaches must have a basic understanding of the game in order to teach kids how to play. Don't assume kids know the rules and terminology of basketball or the basic concepts of the game. Take a few moments in the first few practices to explain these things to kids and use demonstrations and visual cues as much as possible. Utilize this section to help teach the kids the terms and rules of the game along with the basic concepts and strategies.

23. THE BASKETBALL COURT

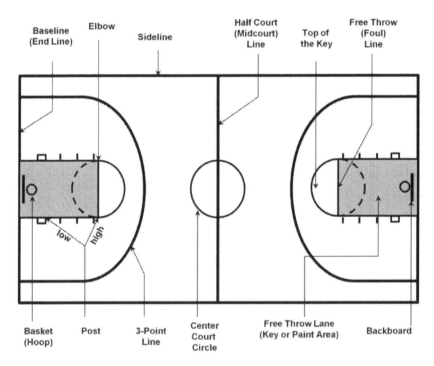

Backboard: The rectangular board behind the rim.

Baseline or End Line: The two "Out of Bounds" lines behind each basket.

Basket or Hoop: An 18 inch metal rim attached to the "Backboard" that the ball is shot through to score.

Center Court Circle: This is the area in the middle of the court that is identified with a circle bisected by the "Half Court Line". This is the area in which "Jump Balls" take place.

Elbow: A term often used to indicate the area of the court where the "Free Throw Line" and side of the "Key" area meet forming a right angle.

Free Throw Lane or Key or Paint Area: A 12-foot wide area extending from the "Baseline" to the "Free Throw Line". This is the area where "Three-second Violations" are applied.

Free Throw Line or Foul Line: A 12-foot-long line that is parallel to and 15 feet from the "Backboard". This is where free throws are shot from.

Inbounds: This is the area within the "Baselines" and "Sidelines" of the court; the active area of the court.

Out of Bounds: The area outside of and including the "Baselines" and "Sidelines".

Post: The name of the sides of the "Free Throw Lane". The area of the post close to the basket is called the "low" post while the area near the free throw line or elbow is called the "high" post. Players also line up along the post during free throw attempts.

Sidelines: The two out of bounds lines that run the length of the court.

Three Point Line: The line surrounding the basket in a semi-circle that is approximately 20-24 feet from the basket depending on the level of play. Shots made from beyond the line are worth three points. Some courts don't have such lines.

Top of the Key: The area near the top of the semi-circle just above the "Free Throw Line".

24. PLAYER POSITIONS

Center: A position typically played by the tallest players who play mainly in the Low Post areas around the basket. They often play in the "Baseline" and "High Post" areas as well, but do not typically play on the perimeter of the court. They are sometimes referred to as "post" players.

Forward: A position typically played by a taller player who plays mainly in the "High Post", "Wing", and "Baseline" areas of the court. "Power" forwards often play in the "Low Post" areas as well.

Guard: A position typically played by shorter players who play mainly on the perimeter of the basket. "Point" guards play in the "Point" area and usually lead the team on offense because they are the better passers and dribblers. "Shooting" guards play on the "Wing" and are usually the better shooters.

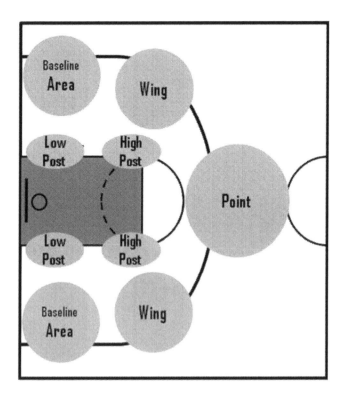

25. OFFENSE TERMINOLGY

Assist: A pass that leads directly to a scored basket.

Bank Shot: A shot that hits the backboard first before "banking" into the basket.

Cut: A quick change of direction by an offensive player to elude a defender and to get open for a pass or a shot.

Dribble or Dribbling: The act of using one's hand to repeatedly bounce the ball onto the court. It's the only legal way for players to both maintain possession of the ball and move around the court.

Drive: A quick movement toward the basket while dribbling the ball in an effort to score or make an assist.

Fake: A deceptive move with or without the ball used to throw a defender off balance and allow an offensive player to shoot, pass, or receive a pass with less defensive pressure. Offensive players typically use shot fakes, pass fakes, and jab steps to accomplish this.

Fast Break: An offensive strategy in which a team attempts to advance the ball down the court as quickly as possible and out run the defense. This usually leads to the defense being temporarily outnumbered by the offense and gives the offense a better opportunity to score.

Field Goal: A shot that goes into the basket other than during a free throw attempt. They are worth two points from inside the three point line and three points beyond the line.

Half-Court Offense: A basic strategy used by the offense to methodically control possession of the ball while in the frontcourt. This usually involves implementing set plays designed to give the offense better scoring opportunities.

Inbound or Throw-Ins: The act where an offensive player throws the ball from the out of bounds area to a team mate in the inbounds area of the court. This is done after a stoppage of play. Players have 5 seconds to inbound the ball once the official has handed them the ball. If they do not pass the ball within 5 seconds, they will be called for a five-second violation and the other team will gain possession of the ball.

Jab Step: A type of fake in which an offensive player takes a hard step in one direction before quickly moving in the opposite direction. This is used to throw defenders off balance and create space for the offensive player to get open for a shot or pass, or to set a pick for a teammate.

Jump Shot or Jumper: A shot (typically from at least five feet from the basket) that is released after the shooter has jumped straight up into the air.

Jump Stop: A method used by players to allow them to completely stop their forward motion by jumping slightly in the air before firmly planting both feet at the same time.

Layup: A shot taken close to the basket that is usually banked off the backboard and into the basket. It is typically used when driving to the basket.

Offense: The team that has possession of the basketball. This also refers to the offensive strategy used by a team.

Pass: The act of throwing the ball to a teammate.
> **Baseball Pass:** A 1-handed pass using a baseball throwing motion. This is typically used to advance the ball a very long distance – usually during a fast break.
> **Bounce Pass:** A 1 or 2-handed pass that strikes the floor before it reaches the receiver. This is often used to make it harder for defenders to steal or deflect the pass.
> **Chest Pass:** A 2-handed pass thrown in a straight line from the passer's chest to the chest area of the receiver. This is a quick pass used primarily when there are no defenders between players.
> **Overhead Pass:** A 2-handed pass thrown from above the head. This is typically used when a defender is directly in front of the passer or when the pass needs to go a long distance.

Side Pass: A 1-handed pass (usually a bounce pass) where the passer extends their non-pivot foot at an angle to either side, leans heavily to that side, and uses a side-arm throwing motion to deliver the ball. This pass is used to avoid a defender that is guarding the passer.

Pick or Screen: An action by an offensive player in which they use their stationary body to block the path of a teammate's defender. This allows the teammate to move, dribble, or shoot without the defender being able to follow or stop them.

Pivot: A movement by a non-dribbling offensive player in which they have possession of the ball while keeping one foot (pivot foot) in contact with a spot on the floor without it moving from that established spot. As long as the player does not slide the pivot foot from that spot, they are free to move their other foot and their body in any direction. If the player slides their pivot foot from that spot before, shooting, passing, or dribbling, they will be called for a traveling violation. If the player lifts their pivot foot off the ground they will not be called for traveling unless the foot touches the floor again before the player shoots or passes the ball – they cannot dribble once they lift their pivot foot.

Pivot Foot: The foot that must remain on the floor while an offensive player has the ball in a non-dribbling position. If a player gets control of the ball with both feet on the floor, either foot can be used as the pivot foot.

Squaring Up: This refers to the desired position of a player's body when they are shooting the ball. It is accomplished when a player's shoulders and feet are squarely facing the basket during a shot.

Three-point field goal: A made basket from beyond the three-point line.

Triple Threat Position: This is an offensive position a player can use who has not dribbled yet. The offensive player stands with knees flexed, feet slightly wider than shoulder width, and both hands on the basketball held away from the defender. From this position, the offensive player can either 1) shoot, 2) dribble, or 3) pass to a teammate … thereby being a 'triple threat' to the defense.

26. DEFENSE TERMINOLOGY

Blocked Shot: The deflection of a shot by a defender that prevents a field goal from being made.

Defense: The team that does not have possession of the ball and that attempts to prevent the other team (offense) from scoring. This also refers to the defensive strategy used by a team.

Double Team: A defensive strategy in which two defenders guard one player on the opposing team.

Guarding: The act of a player closely defending an offensive player without fouling them. This is done to disrupt the offense and prevent or make it harder for them to shoot, dribble, pass or receive a pass.

Man-to-Man Defense: A defensive strategy in which each defender is assigned to guard a specific player on offense.

Press: A defensive strategy in which pressure is applied to the offense using aggressive guarding and double teams in an attempt to force turnovers. Presses are typically applied when the offense is attempting to inbound the ball in the backcourt ("full court" press) or as soon as the offense crosses the half court line with the ball ("half court" press).

Steal: The act of a defensive player taking the ball from the offense and gaining possession of the ball.

Zone Defense: A defensive strategy in which each defender is responsible for defending a designated area of the court and guarding specific offensive players only when they enter their area.

27. TYPES OF VIOLATIONS

Backcourt Violation (10-Second Rule): A violation that occurs when the offensive team fails to advance the ball past the "Half Court Line" within 10 seconds of gaining possession in the "Backcourt". This is also known as a "10-second violation".

Backcourt Violation (Over-and-Back Rule): A violation that occurs when the offensive team advances the ball past half court into the "Frontcourt", and then dribbles back over half court or touches the ball in the "Backcourt" before the opposing team touches it.

Basket Interference: Similar to goal tending, this is a violation that occurs when 1) the ball is touched while it is on the rim of the basket, entering the basket, or has any portion above the rim and within the circumference of the basket, 2) the basket or net is touched while the ball is on the rim, entering the basket, or has any portion above the rim and within the circumference of the basket, 3) the ball is touched by a player reaching up through the basket before the ball has gone completely through the basket or, 4) the basket is pulled down (using the rim or the net) and then released just before the ball reaches the rim. If the defense commits this violation, the offense is awarded the points for the field goal. If the offense commits this violation, the basket is not counted and the opposing team is given possession of the ball.

Carrying or Palming: A violation committed by a dribbler that involves placing the dribbling hand under the ball and momentarily holding or carrying it during the act of dribbling.

Double Dribble: A violation that occurs when a player dribbles the ball with two hands simultaneously or when a player stops dribbling and then dribbles again.

Five-Second Violation: A violation by an offensive player caused when they maintain possession of the ball for five seconds while being closely guarded by a defender just above the top of key. Defenders must stay within 6 feet of the offensive player for the entire five seconds in order for the violation to be valid. A five-second violation also occurs when an offensive player fails to inbound the ball within five seconds of being handed the ball by the official.

Goal Tending: The act of interfering with a ball that has been shot and is on its downward flight toward the basket, but not on the rim or in the area directly above the rim. This violation is also called if the ball has been shot off the backboard and is subsequently touched before touching the rim or entering the area directly above the rim -- regardless of the flight of the ball. The ball must have a reasonable chance of going in the basket for this violation to be called. If the defense commits this violation, the offense is awarded the points as if the field goal had gone in the basket. If the offense commits this violation, the basket is not counted and the opposing team is given possession of the ball.

Three-Second Violation: A violation in which an offensive player remains within the "Free Throw Lane" or "Paint Area" for more than three seconds at a time. If the player is in the "Lane" and subsequently receives the ball, the three second count starts over.

Traveling or Walking: A violation in which a player is in possession of the ball and illegally moves their pivot foot prior to the start of their dribble or after they stop dribbling. Players in the act of advancing toward the basket (as with a layup) are allowed to take two steps without dribbling. The first step establishes the pivot foot and the second step is taken with the non-pivot foot. A third step would cause the pivot foot to return to the floor resulting in a "Traveling" violation.

28. TYPES OF FOULS

Blocking Foul: The use of a defender's body to illegally prevent an opponent's movement. This is the opposite of a "Charging Foul".

Bonus or Penalty Situation: A situation in which a team has accumulated 7 personal fouls within one half of the game. When this occurs the fouling team is said to be in the "penalty" while the opposing team is said to be in the "bonus". The team in the bonus is awarded a one-and-one free throw opportunity for each subsequent non-shooting foul during the half instead of getting possession of the ball for such fouls. Once a team reaches 10 fouls in one half, the other team is said to be in the "double bonus" where they automatically get 2 free throws instead of the one-and-one for non-shooting fouls.

Flagrant or Intentional Personal Foul: A personal foul (accidental or intentional) that involves excessive or severe contact during a live ball situation. Players that commit such fowls are ejected from the game and the opposing team is awarded two free throw attempts and possession of the ball.

Flagrant Technical Foul: A technical foul that is assessed for unsportsmanlike conduct that is extreme in nature; or for excessive or severe contact during a dead ball situation. Fighting is also considered a "Flagrant Technical Foul". Players that commit such fowls are ejected from the game and the opposing team is awarded two free throw attempts and possession of the ball.

Foul or Personal Foul: Physical contact between players that may result in injury or provide one team with an unfair advantage. They are penalized by a change in possession or free throw attempts for the team that is fouled. If a player is not in the act of shooting they are not awarded any free throw attempts UNLESS the player's team is in a bonus situation in which case one or two free throw attempts are awarded.

Free Throw or Foul Shot: An unguarded shot taken from just behind the Free Throw Line after a foul has been committed. Made free throws count for one point.

One-and-One: A free-throw attempt which, if made, allows the player to get a second free throw attempt. If the first attempt is missed, the missed ball is live and can be rebounded by either team.

Shooting Foul: A personal foul committed against the shooter during the act of shooting. Two free throw attempts (three if beyond the three point line) are awarded when a player is fouled in the act of shooting but misses the shot. If the player makes the shot and is fouled, one free throw attempt is awarded (see "Three Point Play").

Technical Foul or "T": A non-contact foul assessed for unsportsmanlike behavior and for some procedural violations such as having too many players on the court or calling a timeout when none remain. Such fouls can be assessed against any member of the team (on or off the court) or against the team as a whole. The opposing team is awarded a free throw attempt and possession of the ball.

Three Point Play: A play in which an offensive player is fouled while shooting and making a 2-point field goal and subsequently makes the free throw they are awarded.

29. OTHER TERMS

Backcourt: The half of the court in which a team plays defense.

Boxing or Blocking Out: A player's attempt to position his body between his opponent and the basket to have a better chance of securing the rebound.

Dead Ball: A situation in which the ball is not actively in play due to a stoppage by an official, or during the brief period between a made "Field Goal" and the "Inbounding" of the ball back into play.

Defensive Rebound: A rebound secured by a player on the defensive team.

Frontcourt: The half of the court in which a team plays offense.

Jump Ball: The procedure used by officials to start games and to start any overtime periods. This involves the official tossing the ball into the air while two opposing players jump up and attempt to tip the ball to one of their teammates. The jumping players are positioned within the "Center Court Circle" and on their "Backcourt" side of the "Half Court Line". The remaining players are positioned around the "Center Court Circle" in an alternating pattern.

Jump Ball ("Held Ball" Rule): A situation in which players on opposing teams have possession of the ball at the same time. This is also referred to as a "jump ball".

Live Ball: A situation in which the ball is actively in play.

Loose Ball: A ball that is still in play but is not in the possession of either team.

Offensive Rebound: A rebound secured by a player on the offensive team.

Officials: The referees who supervise the game on the court and who control the game clock. Their primary duty is to identify fouls and violations and to impose the appropriate penalties.

One-and-One: The "bonus" free-throw situation awarded for non-shooting fouls after the opposing team exceeds a certain number of team fouls in a half. The person fouled shoots one free throw; if successful, the shooter is awarded a second shot.

Possession: To be holding or in control of the ball.

Possession Arrow: An indicator at the scorer's table that is used to determine which team gains possession of the ball at the beginning of each period and after "Held Ball" situations. The arrow alternates between the teams after the beginning of the game.

Rebound: The act of securing possession of the ball after a missed shot.

Scrimmage: A practice game between two different teams, or between two groups of players from the same team.

Substitute: A player who enters the game to replace a player on the court.

Timeout: When play is temporarily suspended by an official or at the request of a team.

Transition: The shift from offense to defense or from defense to offense.

Turnover: A loss of possession of the ball by means of an turnover, violation, or foul by the offense.

30. CONCLUSION

It takes courage to step forward and volunteer to coach young kids. It represents a huge personal commitment and everyone should be grateful for such selflessness. For the most part everyone is supportive, but please be advised: youth coaches will be vulnerable to criticism, embarrassment and even failure; they will be second-guessed and given unsolicited advice; they will be ignored and ridiculed; they may even be yelled at or threatened. All of these negative elements are things that every coach at every level must face – it comes with the job so be prepared.

The best weapon youth coaches have against negativity is a positive attitude. They must set a positive example at all times and protect the kids from any negative influences. Youth coaches must constantly remind themselves that the happiness and well being of the kids is paramount and that their only obligation is to ensure the happiness and well being of the kids. In many ways they must adopt a child-like attitude and not take things too seriously – especially winning and losing.

Above all else, youth coaches must remember that youth sports belongs to the kids and that they simply need a safe and healthy environment in which to play and have fun. So…just let them play and have fun!

> *"We don't stop playing because we grow old; we grow old because we stop playing." --George Bernard Shaw*

Made in the USA
San Bernardino, CA
10 November 2019